Leonard Low was born in Largo in Fifeshire in 1967. He moved to London in 1988, where he was involved in building trade management for the next 23 years. He has two children, a huge ginger cat called Hamish, a black dog called Lucifer and a rare breed of hens – Scots Dumpys – to look after. A long fascination of the dark side of history led to his first book, *The Weem Witch*, which is now in its third printing. A further book called *Largo's Untold Stories* revealed more obscure, dark secrets, this time from his home village of Largo. A lecturer on the subject of his books and the witch trials in general, Lenny is a witch historian with many artefacts from actual trials and a library full of 17th and 18th century books for his source material. Lenny lives in Leven with his partner Ruth, and stepdaughter Amber.

Lenny says, 'Still an East Fife supporter, but we need to win some games!'

By the same author

The Weem Witch
There Are Such Things!
Largo's Untold Stories

St Andrews' UNTOLD STORIES

LEONARD LOW

Steve Savage
LONDON AND EDINBURGH

Steve Savage Publishers Ltd
The Old Truman Brewery
91 Brick Lane
LONDON
E1 6QL

www.savagepublishers.com

First published in Great Britain by Steve Savage Publishers Ltd 2015

ISBN: 978-1-904246-44-2

Typeset by Steve Savage Publishers
Printed and bound by SRP Ltd, Exeter

MIX
Paper from
responsible sources
FSC® C014540

Acknowledgements

This is the fourth book I have written, but in a way it has been the easiest one to write, for most of the information has been within reach, staring down at me from my archive of 17th and 18th-century books. Previous research has taken me to all corners of Britain in other people's libraries to get what I was after, but with centuries of my family history being directly associated with St Andrews, there's very little I don't have already on the city. But again I have my wee army of friends and followers who make things that little bit easier, I couldn't have got this far without help and information from many secondary sources. I would like to thank as follows ...

The *East Fife Mail*, the *Weekly News*, the *Courier* and the *Fife Free Press*, for all the coverage and interviews given during my last book, about Largo, Scottish Psych Research for having me, and the *Fortean Times*. Many thanks to Ian Muirhead, Stephen Gilfeather, Bruce Marshall, John van Dieken, Greg Stewart and Kyle, Willie Maclean and Walter and Cath, Jamie (up the Rams) Rowbotham, John the Bet, David (Puff) Baxter, Margo, Irish Jocky and Ian Pirie, Amber and Dylan. Great thanks to The Scottish Society for Psychichal Research.
Many thanks to the Fife Council Archaeologist Douglas Spiers for his time and thoughts on the Greyfriars

dig. Thanks to Lyle Slovick for letting me use his research on the rabbit wars.

The Low clan ... David, Linda and my two little big ones Callum and Kirsty Low and Amber Sinclare-Case. Also Cousin Brenda, Uncle Fitz's niece.

I used to travel every month from London, England, to Lundin Links in Scotland to do my Weem Witch tour in Pittenweem. With me on the train journey would be Hamish, my enormous ginger cat. I'm now permanently in Leven and Hamish is still here by my side. I did a book signing in St Andrews' Waterstones for my last book on Largo: I got out the car and a huge crowd was there ... but not for me! A cat in St Andrews had a book out, he's big and ginger ... his name is Hamish! I was upstaged and outsold by a ginger cat called Hamish!

A lot of this book had to be translated from very old 16th-century records and diaries, wearing white gloves to protect such precious books. It was incredibly hard work and very time-consuming to read through and translate the Old Scots language into today's English. Sometimes I was on it twenty hours a day, and many nights in bed I've closed my eyes and all I can see are pages and pages of old script written in Old Scots.

Insomnia I suffer terribly from, and to be close to me you must put up with eccentric sleeping hours, and a bit of the darkness that follows with me and my art and ghostly hobbies. My love to Ruth Sinclare-Case who creeps around and manages to ignore the madness that consumes me when I'm on to something. Normal relationships usually have room for nice restaurants and scenic pubs – on my journeys it's ruined castles and haunted houses. How about thinking you're going for a country pub lunch and instead being upside down cleaning out an old Druid sacrificial pool to see what's in there at the bottom — romantic or what? Without Ruth's understanding I would certainly be in an asylum somewhere! High fives to Pittenweem and St Andrews Primary 7s who now get taught the Weem Witch in class and let me lecture to them. Great kids, whose mums should be proud of the intelligent questions they dig up for me.

Many thanks to those who continue coming on my Weem Witch tour and invite me to lecture. I am still battling to promote a lasting monument to the "Weem Witches". Some fruit may come of this — if you want to help, contact me below.

To all the readers who have kept me going over the last three books, here is book four with more to come.

THANK YOU

Leonard Low
Leven
Aug 10 ... 3 am
(Can't sleep again, seeing pages of sunken fishing boats)

To contact WEEM WITCH TOURS or the author:

07766553377
lennyweemwitches@hotmail.co.uk

Contents

Introduction   11

1 Muckross ... The Land of Boars   15

2 The Man who Ate his Fingers   27

3 The Formidable Rise and Fall of David Beaton   38

4 The Burning of George Wishart   45

5 Two Men with a Destiny of Witchcraft   54

6 Fornicators, Fornicating Fornicators!   65

7 The Plague Years   101

8 The Brutal Murder of Archbishop Sharp   109

9 They Sleep with the Fish   120

10 The Rabbit War of 1801–21   153

11 First World War VC – John Ripley   158

12 Nazi Bombs Fall on St Andrews   164

13 The St Andrews Sausage Slaughter   168

14 The Return of the 15th-Century Monks   173

15 Alphonse Capone "Scars" the Old Course   178

16 The Return of St Andrew   186

17 Today's St Andrews   187

Sources   190

Picture credits   192

Introduction

When I was growing up in the small village of Upper Largo in Fife in the 1970s, a regular visitor to the house would be my great-uncle Fitz.

Fitz was my grandfather's brother: Fitz Mason was his name. His arrival would usually warrant the delivery and the very welcome smell of delicious fish and chips all wrapped up in newspapers, from the Anstruther chippy along the coast.

He was a smartly-dressed, very tall, kind man, with a chivalry about him from a more courteous time and age. A man with a handshake as strong as iron – outstretched in greeting, his hand would crush the very soul from you no matter how you would steel yourself for it. (I can vouch for that even in my thirties.) A brilliant storyteller with a lifetime of fantastic dramatic tales of his time in the Canadian wastes, hanging criminals, problems with polar bears, snakes and elephant hunting in Africa – he owned a shrunken head from the Amazon – and he had many stories which would be continually regaled to me in front of a log fire after dinner, and then later we would be battling it out over a game of chess.

I would be ten years old, Fitz in his seventies. This amazing man was born in St Andrews, Scotland, in 1908, and set off for the cold Canadian wastes to join the Hudson Bay Company in 1926. He left them and joined the Royal

Canadian Mounted Police, where he met cases of cannibalism in the Arctic wastes; he hanged a man wanted for murder, tried his luck gold prospecting in the Klondike, went to South America and got involved in diamond mining, then off to Africa and platinum dredging in the British Cameroons. In all, a very interesting active life, but it all started in St Andrews, and so did his stories.

He told me about the hard days he had at St Andrews school, where he was regularly beaten by his teachers, as was everyone in his class! But one particular teacher in 1919 was most brutal to them. This man had served on the front in France for four years during the First World War. His job before the war had been that of a teacher, but now after the horrors he had witnessed he was a much changed man. There was this instance where Fitz's brother William had an altercation with the teacher and he wrestled William to the floor and put his knee to his neck, held it tight till my great-uncle William passed out, then dragged him to his seat in class and carried on the lesson!

Another pupil was beaten and bullied by this man as he had a sickly stature. The boy eventually died at home, and the teacher was seen as blameless ... but Fitz and others at the school knew better! Fitz was soon off to Canada. But he swore one day he would be back in St Andrews, where he would hunt down this teacher ... and kill him! He certainly came home again, years later and went secretly to carry out his oath, but he told me someone had beaten him to it. The teacher was already dead!

Fitz would outlive his own brothers and sisters, then my father and my sister – he was 95 when he died. But in his nineties his loneliness in having no one his own age to talk to really affected him. I would visit him in his retirement flat in St Andrews with my brother David, a bottle of 12-year-old Macallan for a visa. Again his stories were fresh and his memory crisp judging by the details he carried – and still a terrific handshake! He passed away in 2007, sat down in his house and never got up again. Fitz is now with my grandparents, my mother and a centuries-long line of ancestors born from St Andrews stock. He lies in Strathkinnes cemetery with the rest of the Mason storytellers. And this is where this book starts, a book on St Andrews, mainly from Fitz and his tales, the city's humble beginnings from a shipwreck containing the Greek monk Regulus and his followers with some selected bones of Jesus's first disciple Andrew. The boat wrecked itself in the local bay and would set the seeds of Christianity in the East coast of Scotland and eventually form this magnificent city.

This book covers the darker past of St Andrews. I work my way through the years and centuries in layers like an archaeologist gently turning over finds to piece together a story. My two previous books *The Weem Witch* and *Largo's Untold Stories* show how I thrive in the darkness of history and dig deep to expose the very interesting but not so pretty past.

I always found the stories Fitz told fascinating and still hold them dear, alongside the tales he told me I have chased up the documented facts from early sources. In history the little pieces of fact that are not usually so acclaimed by other writers are left behind for bigger stories. Some writers continue to use the same tales from the same sources, another new book bringing absolutely nothing new to the reader, a repetition of every book before it. I like to dig deep to find important enough events connected to St Andrews, however strange they may seem. But also to add a chapter to St Andrews' great and rich history that hasn't been told before.

In this volume of St Andrews' past, I carry on from my Great-Uncle Fitz a tradition from the many generations of the Mason family born here, and regale you now after much research with *St Andrews' Untold Stories* ...

Do enjoy ...

Leonard (Mason) Low
Leven

Chapter 1

Muckross ... The Land of Boars

Born in the first century in the village of Bethsaida, on the Sea of Galilee, Andrew was a fisherman by trade, as was his brother Peter.

Andrew was a follower of the Christian prophet John the Baptist, who preached by the river Jordan. He and his brother would meet another preacher one day who was related to John the Baptist and follow him with several others as disciples. They followed this man and obeyed his commands and teachings. This man was called Jesus, and claimed to be "the son of God"!

Jesus would go on to upset the Jewish priests with his claims, and be arrested; he would eventually be put to death nailed on a cross with two common thieves on a hill at Jerusalem.

Later his disciples would give out the words Jesus had told them, spreading the words and teachings of Christianity. Andrew preached along the coast of the Black Sea and as far as Kiev. He founded the See of Byzantium in 38AD, installing a bishop; the diocese would eventually become the hugely successful trade centre of Constantinople.

Andrew would meet his end in the city of Patras in Greece, where the ruler Aigeates took grave offence to the converting of his wife by Andrew to Christianity. He had him put to death on an X-shaped cross, tying his legs and arms and hanging him upside down. He was 80 years old and took three days to die.

Andrew's bones were at first laid to rest in the city of Patras until the year 357 when the Roman Emperor Constantius II deposited the bones in the Byzantine capital's Church of the Holy Apostles.

On the 29th of October 370AD, the Greek abbot Regulus (his name meant little king) left the city of Patras where he was based, and got aboard a boat, which he commanded, with seventeen other monks and three nuns, and set off on a journey, simply due to a vision he had had, where St Andrew himself had called to Regulus to take his body and teachings to the end of the earth. After a few days at sea Regulus had stopped the boat at the city of Constantinople (Byzantium) and taken on board some of the bones of St Andrews. They were placed in an elaborate box for the journey. The box contained ...

One of the arm bones,
Three of the fingers,
A tooth,
Three toes,
One of the knee caps.

These fragments were carried in the box as the boat made its two-year journey out of the Mediterranean, round Spain, through the English Channel and up the east coast of Britain until it hit heavy seas around the Scottish coast.

The boat was having great difficulty and finally beached on the rocks. It smashed to pieces, and all belongings and cargo were lost. This miserable soaking group of stragglers looked up at sheer cliffs as they picked themselves off the beach. The box of St Andrews' relics was the only thing they managed to salvage from the doomed wrecked boat.

They took refuge in a natural cave on the beach as the storm raged around them (now below Kirk Hill) but their plight had not gone unnoticed. The local tribesmen out hunting had spotted the ship's demise on the beach. This area was known as "Muckross", otherwise translated as "Headland of the Boars"*. It was a marshland that was used by the local Celtic Pictish king Hergust for hunting game. No significance was given to this area bar the king's lodgings for his hunters. He found the sea-wrecked stragglers and they aroused his pity. He offered them his hunting palace nearby as a place for them to rest and recover, so saddened was he by their story.

The religion in this Fife area of Pictland was druidic in nature, a mysterious almost forgotten religion. Because the Picts and Celts held no passion for writing, almost all on the druids' nature was lost to us in the years gone by. What little we know was written by others who invaded this country and made mention of them in memoirs of their own tongue. Julius Caesar wrote that the Celtic people "affirm that they are all descended from a common father, Dis, and say that this is the tradition of the druids". The Picts and Celts held religious festivals to hail the gathering of crops, one was later known as "Lammas" (which is still a celebration of sorts in St Andrews today).

* "muc" meaning sow and "ross" meaning promontory

Fire played its part in the beliefs of the druids also. To imitate the course of the sun, to go right-handed holding a torch of fire was to perform a ritual to bring beneficial results. Fire, representing the sun going in its circle of the day, was carried in blazing torches around cattle, housing, corn and people to ensure wellbeing. To go left-handed and anti-clockwise (widdershins) was a violation of the order and was seen to bring harm. (This ritual is sometimes carried out by fishermen today before sailing; fishermen with the risks present over the years are still very superstitious people.)

Standing stones are all that can be seen today dating from the druidic teachings of old. The Romans talked of sacrifices at these locations, and we can guess weddings and religious offerings were also the norm here in those dark-like days. Again the frustration is that we just don't know what the stone monoliths in areas like Lundin Links actually represented. Stone circles like the Ring of Brodgar in Orkney, Balquhain at Inverurie and Tomnaverie at Tarland are but a few of the examples around Scotland we can still view today.

Regulus interested King Hergust in his religious teachings. He allowed him to use his hunting palace as a permanent home and endorsed Christianity around the druid shrines and holy places around the area. The historian Fordun mentions "Hergust having founded a church or cell in the form of a monastery for his people. The holy man Regulus went out like Christ preaching the words of eternal life to the ignorant barbarians accompanied by some assistants and translators." One such area, just outside St Andrews, is Dunino.

It is a V-necked valley hidden in a thick forest, with a burn running the distance through it. This was an ancient place of worship for the Picts and the druid teachers of old, where from a height the shaman could preach to the pagans below waiting in the valley.

A son of the Dunino Manse, Dr Charles Roger, born in 1824, a man well known in Scotland for his contributions to literature, was instrumental in discovering the particularities of the religious area. He cleaned away the soil and moss from the side of the drop to the river, uncovering a deep pot-hole with a cut-out footrest carved into the rock. It is believed to be the sacrifice pool, the cut-out being in the perfect position to put one's foot to hold down a victim while making the blood offering to whichever gods required that. Sharpening marks on the nearby rocks suggest this was so, and that the pool was to collect the offerings of blood!

A small stone circle was in existence outside the forest in a field which the druids held sacred. But with the intervention of Regulus and his teachings, Christianity in its basic form was taught here and all the evidence points to the druidic teachings being supplanted by Christianity. The circle of stones was dug up and they were used in the building of the nearby church, which stands metres from where the stones were positioned. A square druid altar stone was pulled into the church grounds and converted into a sundial, and is still to be seen here.

Today the druid valley can be found untouched by modernization. The sacrificial pool is still there. You can visualise the druid priest killing the sacrifice over the pool, letting the blood spurt and flow and then casting the body over the edge into the river ten metres below, watched by a cheering crowd of pagan supporters. Squeeze yourself down the narrow pathway to the base of the valley floor and Pictish knot carvings may be viewed on the cliff face.

The Dunino sacrificial hole, on a cliff top in the den.

A small cave is located beneath the cliff and one can visualise the shamans resting in there. It is central to the area, and must have been important for whoever sat here. More carvings can be found, a facial carving of a bearded figure, probably a bit more modern than the knot carving, but possibly representing the green man of the forest, another god they held in high esteem. A very high crucifix is carved into the rock face three metres high in Celtic style. This could be from Regulus' people, or as history here states from the Culdees, who preached here after Regulus, and followed an early monastic form of Christianity.

Dunino is a place the author highly recommends the reader to find for him or herself: it holds its mysterious past well, and if you stand by the river and look up at the cliff face, you can certainly picture the druid priests at work here and the followers of Regulus. It's a classic place where you can see evidence of one religion supplanting another.

Up high on the clifftops adjacent to the sacrifice pool, there is a deep hole cut into the rock where, say, a wooden crucifix could be stood, and a preacher could do his work.

Modern pagans today still make pilgrimages to the area bypassing the Christian church that sits by the farm road on the way to the den. While I was there on my visit, a family had spent the night down there. They had come from Switzerland. Many ribbons and unnameable flowers (and very interesting cigarettes!) had been tied to the branches of the trees, giving the place a creepy feel to it. It is good to know the pagan shrine here is still held in awe for some.

King Hergust was, for a barbarous druidical heathen, a wise and charitable man, for hearing of the lonely group of stragglers washed up from the shipwreck with their religious objects, he set them to be his guests. Hergust treated them kindly, fed and clothed them and saw that Christianity would be a great advertisement for the welfare of his people. Becoming a convert himself, he insisted that his kingdom follow his example and dispel forever the power of the druids and their barbarous traditions. Regulus lived another thirty-two years after his forced arrival in Muckross. By the time of his death Christianity had taken hold in Fife. At that time the Picts and Scots were separate Kingdoms. The Pictish monarchy extended more to the lowlands and the North East part of the country. The other side of the Grampian Mountains and over the Highlands and the Western isles made up the homeland to the Scots.

The Fife Picts were described by the Graeco-Egyptian geographer Claudius Ptolemy (ca 100–170AD) as two separate tribes, the Veniconi to the East and Horseti to the West. He describes them as fearsome painted people, both men and women heavy in tattoos. With thirteen such tribes in Caledonia (Scotland) these warlike people gave the Romans such a problem that they could not properly subdue them, building Hadrian's Wall and then the Antonine Wall to defend themselves from them.

Regulus had died, but his legacy and followers carried on the faith. A church was built in the Muckross area after his death, and the bones of St Andrews were taken to the Pictish capital of Kilrule (near Markinch today). Muckross was renamed Kylrymont and became a centre of religious teachings as more churches were commissioned to be built.

Around the year 832AD*, the Picts' king was Hungus (Oengust or Unust, born early 9th century) who, along with his Scots nephew Kenneth MacAlpin (who was son of the King of Scots), were engaged in warfare against the Saxon king of Northumberland called Athelstane. A large war party had invaded the Northumbrian lands expecting to meet Athelstane and surprise him in his own lands. The Pict army was never threatened, but went rampaging through the farms and rich holdings, taking their wealth back over the border.

On returning from an attack on the Northumbrian lands, loaded with captured gold and immense booty, it was found that the Northumbrian army had been raiding the Pict lands at the same time!

The Picts were surprised by King Athelstane's army near Haddington and a battle ensured. The Picts were heavily outnumbered by the Northumbrians and although

* Many historians are confused over this date, some giving it as the year 800, others around 832; with the Pictish King Hungus getting three versions of his own name – Unust or Oengust. Again the Picts having word of mouth records plays havoc with dates. What is undisputed is the battle and the outcome happened: just the dates are obscured.

they fought skilfully and ferociously, as was their reputation, the greater numbers began to sway the battle. Axe
and spear left a battlefield of gore and shattered limbs,
sword met sword after spears were lost and thrown. The
ground was bloody, but neither foe would yield possession.
They fought till nightfall until both armies backed off to
lick their wounds and wait for the light of morning to
commence this bloody brawl.

The Picts had the worst of it: many of their warriors
were wounded or dead. Hungus expected the Northumbrian
host would now sweep over the Picts with full force the
minute the sun rose, so outnumbered had they seemed to be
on the field. It was a sorry time and the situation was one of
worry and defeat.

In amongst the baggage of the Pictish warriors was a
box of bones containing parts of Andrew, the fisherman
from Galilee. In the Scottish wars it was the tradition to
carry holy relics or for druidic shamans to show blessings
to the gods before committing battle. (Robert the Bruce,
500 years after this date, would have the bones of St Fillan
on the field of Bannockburn resting in a small box to give
his men saintly guidance in the forthcoming battle with
the English. Bruce was outnumbered himself by the
enemy's strength at least four to one.)

But as dawn broke the frosty night and warriors
prepared themselves for the coming fight, it so happened
that the stratus formation of clouds in the sky was parted
by a gentle breeze. The clouds moved into an unmistakable
cloud formation of a cross in the sky – white cloud on a
blue background – it was the image of the cross that St
Andrews himself had been martyred on!

Hungus saw the sign in the sky and saw it as a potential sign from St Andrew himself and urged his troops that God was indeed on his side. They all raised their heads to the sky and witnessed this sign.

The dawn attack that was expected that morning never came; the Northumbrians had many dead and wounded too, and after the rash clash of arms the previous day they were obviously wary of their vicious foes. Skirmishing was all that took place that day as each commander with his council sought to get the better of his foe. As night came again the stalemate remained unbroken, but amongst the Picts now a newfound belief roused their energies.

The morning of another day came and instead of waiting for the greater Northumbrian host to make its move, the Pict army, bolstered by the sign of St Andrew, attacked full-on, and with axes, swords and spears they shattered the vanguard of the enemy, killing Athelstane himself. The Saxons, seeing their leader hacked dead and bloody, ran from the field as the Picts leapt upon them and cut them down. Victory was with the Picts. But the honour was bestowed on the cross of St Andrew.

The historian Fordun (a secular priest who documented Scottish history ... born around 1350, died 1384) says that Regulus' followers and monks obtained a grant of certain lands in the neighbourhood on the account of the signal of assistance from St Andrew that granted huge riches to Hungus in the expedition against the Saxons. He bestowed great gifts to Regulus' church, such as chalices, basins and the image of Christ made in gold and silver, and a box made from gold (a reliquary) to hold the fragments of bone that had been brought to these shores by Regulus. He granted all tithes of the corn and cattle within the realm to the church and exempted churchmen from appearing before temporal judges. He also ruled that the St Andrew cross was to be the cognisance of the Pict nation in all their wars.

Today the coat of arms of St Andrews has the cross of St Andrew with a tusked boar underneath an oak tree representing the two great names the area had.

In 843 it came about that Kenneth MacAlpin became King of Scots, including the Picts. In the Pictish lands there

The Regulus tower and parish church (roof missing) where St Andrew's bones resided

was always conflict in the border lowlands between the Picts and the Angles and Saxons of Northumbria – a constant attrition of the stock of Pict warriors – but then another foe arrived on the east coast. The Viking hordes.

The Picts rose bravely under King Drustin to fight this new enemy, the Vikings landing in galleys around the coast with a ferociousness to match the Picts as more warriors went down to this new army from across the sea. They managed to repel them but at huge loss.

What happened next is clouded in the history of Scotland – it is very unclear what exactly took place. But King Kenneth called a meeting with the new Pictish King Drustin and his lieutenants, in which a dinner was planned with all the honours a king could bestow on a royal guest. During the meal a fight broke out, and by the end of the mêlée the Pictish king and his sons and successors were slain and murdered over the tables set for them.

The Picts had been so weakened by wars on all sides that they had no officers to avenge their fallen kings, so Kenneth stepped in and managed the Pict nations himself. He installed one of his nobles Fifus Duffus into the realm which took his name "Fife" – the Duffus family became the thanes of Fife. With the title came the hereditary right of crowning the Kings of Scotland under the name McDuff. Now the combined force of the remnants of the Picts and the Scots under the white-cross banner on a blue background rose as a unified Scottish army, and defended the coasts of the homeland as one, protecting the land from Viking invaders from Denmark, and those from England.

The Pictish capital at Abernethy was moved to Kilrymont, and Kilrymont was then rechristened St Andrews, where the saint's bones were now themselves given pride of place in the chapel of St Rule. St Andrew was adopted by the Scots nation as our patron saint. After the wreck of the Pictish kingdom it was more of an incorporation and union of the two nations than a forced merger. The two nations had fought common enemies for centuries, the Romans, the ancient Britons, Jutes, Angles, Northumbrian Saxons – all had been fought back across the borders. The two families were also united by marriage. By King Kenneth destroying what was left of the Pictish monarchy he gained a unified Scotland ... It is him we Scots today must thank for our great nation. But importantly to this book, it's where St Andrews got its name and significance in being a seat of religious learning.

Chapter 2

The Man who Ate his Fingers

The years went past as did Scotland's succession of kings, and St Andrews grew more and more as a centre of religious worship. More money was bestowed on the building of more churches. The Greek preacher Regulus was also known as "Riaghail" which again was shortened to "Rule". A tower and church were built in his memory, and as the building continued it also gained a worldwide audience. There was a traffic of sightseers on their travels making a pilgrimage to see the holy bones of St Andrews. Royalty visited, leaving jewels and money as offerings ... Christianity was becoming a big business.

1112 ... a Parish church was built by Bishop Turgot: Church of the Holy Trinity.

Around 1127... St Rule church with tower was built, a tall square building 153 steps high. (33 metres high)

1140 ... Became a Royal Burgh under King David I.

1162 ... St Andrews Cathedral built.

1200 ... St Andrews Castle built by Bishop Roger (son of the Earl of Leicester).

1274 ... Dominican Friary built by Bishop Wishart. (Its remains can be seen in South Street.)

1296 ... Edward I of England occupies St Andrews Castle.

1296 ... William Wallace takes it.

1303 ... Edward I visits with his wife Queen Eleanor. He leaves a gift of an elaborate gold bracelet set in jewels, to be placed on the arm bone of St Andrew.

1336 ... Edward III has occupation of the castle.

1336 ... The Scottish regent Andrew Moray (son of Wallace's fellow general Moray who died at the battle of Stirling Bridge in 1297) captures the castle from the English ... he dismantles the castle to stop the English using it.

(An English monk at this time described the Scots' eating habits. Monk Ranulph Higden noted that the Scots fed more in flesh, fishes, white meat and with fruits, kale. A recent excavation of bodies from a 14th-century graveyard in Aberdeen gave some startling insights into medieval life in Scotland. Of the 207 unearthed and studied, 58 percent died before their 18th birthday, and half of those died before the age of six. Fewer than 25 percent of the adults reached middle age and very few reached old age. Diseases such as tuberculosis were rife and all skeletons showed damage to bones only usually found with the lifting of heavy weights.)

In 1371 David II of Scotland died. He died without a direct heir, as he had no children to succeed him. Therefore his nephew Robert Stewart took the throne, to become Robert II. King Robert would last only 14 years before illness took hold so he passed it over to his brother John to rule.

Now the last John who sat on the throne of Scotland was King John Balliol. In 1292 he was chosen as king from fourteen other claimants and four years later he would be deposed by Edward I in disgrace – deposed by the very man who chose him!

Edward had continually made jest of King John Balliol, he even once demanded John come in person to London to appear in court over an unpaid wine bill left over from the previous Scots king, Alexander III. That was a three-week journey for a wine bill from someone else who was dead! He finally rebelled after England went to war with France, Edward demanding Scots armies to fight for him. A battle ensued between the Scots and English, but at home the Scots didn't think much of King John either, many not supporting him (the Bruce clan for example). At Dunbar his meagre forces met the English in battle and were soundly defeated. He had his titles humiliatingly ripped from him by the English king at Montrose in 1296. His crown, royal insignia and his surcoat were taken, and this gained him the name "the Toom Tabard", meaning empty coat. He was an unlucky and weak king who divided Scotland in loyalty. He ended his days in France as an outcast, although his supporters still fought his cause back in Scotland (William Wallace, Andrew Moray). His humiliation in front of King Edward I was a memory that would cut deep in the Scottish heritage, with mistakes no one wanted to see repeated. To many King John was a disaster for the country. While resistance against England continued in his name, he never took any interest in the Scottish throne again.

As a result of all this, John was seen as a very unlucky name for a king, so John Stewart was advised by his bishops and officers to change his name to a better suited one ... and he was crowned King Robert III in 1390.

Robert III was unfortunate to have been named "John", but he was even more unfortunate in the state of his physical appearance. Sir Walter Scott wrote about him ... "He was lame in body and feeble in mind – well meaning, pious, benevolent and just, but totally disqualified from want of personal activity and mental energy to hold the reins of government over a fierce and unmanageable people."

Robert had taken a fall from a horse badly in his youth, his body never recovered enough to be agile again. His weakness was well known and embarrassing. His brother the Duke of Albany soon took command, with Robert's position nothing but a puppet king. The nobles in the kingdom paid their courtesies to him as the arbiter of the kingdom's destiny. But at length a rival appeared, in the shape of Robert III's eldest son David, the Duke of Rothesay, whose envious eyes craved the power that one day by right would become his. He had no patience to wait for his day of royalty. He became jealous of the power his uncle the Duke of Albany held, when he was the next in line to the throne after his father. Feeling that he had enough support with the nobles, he thought himself able to usurp his uncle and rule now! His disrespect to his uncle did not go unnoticed, but there was a kingdom to run, so for the time being noises of dissent were ignored. However the Duke of Albany was not a man to jest with!

The young duke David Stewart plotted his succession but with a grave naivety transformed his friends in court to enemies with his overbearing character. His uncle was not long in hearing rumours. David was already betrothed to the daughter of the Earl of March, a marriage arranged by his uncle. But romance turned to rebellion when he ungallantly deserted her and wedded the daughter of the Earl of Douglas instead, who offered a larger dowry. His insult and dealings with the Douglas's clan would result in future turmoil and war!

The duke's eccentric and ill-handed dealings with his father's subjects gave Albany no choice but to deal with him personally. Before it could get out of hand, further action was taken to bring this matter to a dramatic close. His conduct in court was seen as a direct assault on the crown and the father of David, King Robert III, was easily persuaded by his brother Albany to warrant the arrest of his own son because of his behaviour.

It was agreed to arrest the young duke to curb his distemper and foolhardy behaviour before more damage could be done. He was found just outside St Andrews and was apprehended and arrested at a place called Struthers.

He was taken to the formidable St Andrews Castle, and incarcerated in the bottle dungeon there. (The bottle dungeon is a remarkable structure cut into the ground rock of the North West Tower. It is a mined pit! Cut through metres of rock deep down to form a bottle-necked dungeon, it is 7.5 metres deep. The neck is 2 metres in diameter and about 2.5 metres deep. Below this the dungeon widens to reach a diameter of about 5 metres, a dark and airless cavern with no sewage outlet, everything into here has to be lowered down via a rope! A jail with absolutely no hope of escape, a miserable pit where food would be thrown to the stinking wretches below, full of excrement, disease and filth. (It can still be viewed today, although you can't go into it!) The dungeon was a terrible place to end up in, as we shall see later on from others in the future who shared this living hell!

But he was still the next heir to the throne and it was a huge headache for Albany what to do with him. David Stewart still had powerful friends in court, although he had alienated others, but to release him could cause problems. It was deemed that Albany should keep a closer eye on him.

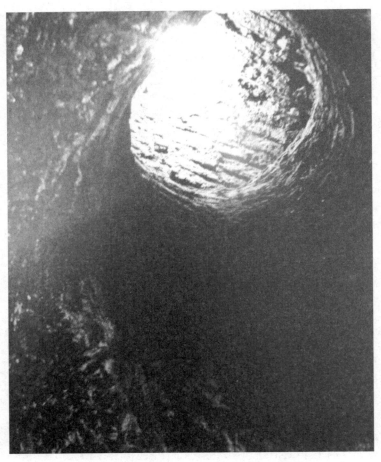

A rare photograph of 1922 from inside the St Andrews bottle dungeon looking up – what David would have seen while jailed inside.

The duke was taken in chains to Falkland Castle later that year. This was the castle where his uncle Albany resided. The dungeons of the castle were underground at the bottom of a tower. His cries for leniency and his wails of sorrow from the dungeons there could not be heard by the regent in his splendid rooms above (or perhaps he chose not to hear them!) but wail and cry he no doubt did. The jailors closed the doors on it. After a long while things went quiet from the young duke's cell ... very quiet!

Who found the wretch is unimportant, but within a few weeks the heir to the Scottish throne was found dead in his cell. It was said that he starved to death; and that the wasted figure in his last days of life had resorted to eating the flesh from his own fingers for sustenance. Hector Boece, the 15th-century historian, wrote that the prince was confined in the tower at Falkland Castle and left entirely without food, that his life was sustained for some time by crumbs and oatcakes which were dropped through the crevices in the roof of his prison by a tender-hearted woman from the neighbourhood, who also fed him breast milk through a straw; but it wasn't enough*. When his emaciated body was later inspected after the prince was dead, it was found that Prince David Stewart, the heir to Scotland, near the point of starvation in his utter neglect, had eaten the flesh from his fingers before he died.

It was said his uncle had wanted him removed from the path of his ambitions and left him to rot in his cell. His uncle Albany and his brother-in-law the Earl of Douglas were openly charged with his murder and brought before the Estates in Edinburgh 16th May 1402. They were

* The tower that the prince was kept in has disappeared under constructions over the years, mainly by James II in 1459. In a recent issue of the *Courier* a page covered a story on the ruins of Lindores Abbey, where archaeologists plan to pinpoint the resting body of the Duke of Rothesay, the son of Robert III, and determine how he actually died. Will they find teeth marks on the bones of his fingers?

examined on this charge and acquitted by the unanimous voice of Parliament with consent of the boy's father, King Robert himself. But who was pulling the king's strings?

The death of the young duke and heir to the throne of Scotland, was declared by Parliament "to have been caused by the hand of God and by no other means", such was Albany's influence over Parliament.

The weak king Robert III, fearing for his other son James, sent him for his own safety to France away from his dominating uncle. But disaster was never far behind this decision. English ships intercepted the Scottish prince's ship and he was to be detained in an English prison for the next 23 years. It was too much for Robert III. His enfeebled body through sickness sped quickly to an early grave, a broken-hearted man and a superseded monarch. Albany now had no opponent to block him: he ruled as before with an iron fist till his death in 1420. Today he lies in Dunfermline Abbey.

James would be released from his English prison in 1425, becoming King James I of Scotland. He never forgot the treatment of his brother, and set out to arrest and execute the sons of Albany for treason, finally destroying the power of the Albany family forever.

1385–1401 ... Bishop Walter Trail rebuilds the castle.

1393 ... Robert de Montrose, a devout and energetic builder of the religious seats in St Andrews, a lord of Parliament and an abbot of the Cathedral. His teachings were strict and he reformed the discipline of the other canons ... upsetting a few along the way. Thomas Plater was one who could take no more of this bully and his teachings, so resolved to murder him. Waiting in the shadows he made his move one rainy night, jumping out and stabbing Robert with a dirk hidden in his robes. He was about to enter the staircase leading to the canons' accommodation, and with his screams of pain the other deacons and monks were quick to the brutal scene. Robert was mortally wounded but lived three days, long enough to identify his assassin as Thomas Plater. Thomas admitted all as his victim died, after three days' agony. Thomas was condemned to perpetual solitary imprisonment: it was the bottle dungeon for him. It was a fate more dreaded than death itself, languishing in that stinking purgatory. The records state he did not survive long down there.

1408 ... John Reseby ... one of the first of many religious martyrs burnt at the stake in St Andrews. He was found to be a heretic who supported the doctrines of John Wyclif. (John Wycliff was an early English philosopher and lay preacher, a dissident of the Catholic Church whose translation of the Bible was to influence the Authorised Version. Died 1384.) The movement of protest against the Catholic Church had started.

1413 ... St Andrews University founded.

1429 ... Hugh Kennedy takes 800 Scotsmen to fight beside Joan of Arc in France; after 15 years of fighting he returns to St Andrews as Provost of the Chapel of St Mary.

1433 ... Paul Craw, a physician from Bohemia, was burnt as a heretic who spoke out. A brass ball was nailed in his mouth lest he utter a declaration against the Catholic Church. Paul was burnt at the Mercat Cross in St Andrews.

1451 * ... James III born in St Andrews Castle

1453 ... John Earl of Mar is baptised at the cathedral ... He is a brother of James III ... The Earl of Mar later fell under the king's suspicion for consulting with witches and sorcerers in 1479 on how to shorten the king's days. (But

* This date is argued over by historians.

otherwise the king was very wary on the influence Mar had over James's own nobles.) On such a charge, elaborately stated, Mar was bled to death in his own lodgings at Craigmillar Castle without trial or conviction. Twelve women and four so-called wizards of obscure rank were burnt immediately at Edinburgh to give credence to the earl's trumped up guilt. (This is one of Scotland's earliest witch trials. The story of poor David Stewart is mirrored here, with witchcraft being the excuse to get rid of a troublesome royal relative.)

1522 ... James Beaton is made Archbishop of St Andrews ... begins the persecution of Scottish Protestants, finding the preachers Patrick Hamilton and George Buchanan guilty of heresy. George managed to escape St Andrews Castle, but Patrick was made an example of and burnt in front of the Salvator church. He was guilty of preaching Martin Luther's work. (Hamilton was son of Patrick Hamilton of Kincavil, a nephew of the Earl of Arran ... not long after the burning, a man by the name of Forrest was also led to the stake for asserting that Hamilton was a martyr not a traitor. This is how any seditious talk was dealt with.)

1539 ... David Beaton, nephew of the Archbishop James Beaton, succeeds to his uncle's position, now vacant ... he becomes Cardinal Beaton.

St Andrews Cathedral today – castle in background.

Chapter 3

The Formidable Rise and Fall of David Beaton

David Beaton became a cardinal in 1538 and took over his uncle's position in 1539. His base and home were at St Andrews Castle.

David Beaton was one of the first Scottish primates to rise so high, and also one of the last! He was of strong character, a forceful, grim and very cunning man. A patriot with resolute attachment to the ancient Catholic beliefs, a true defender of the faith and through a much troubled unsettled period of war and politics in Scotland he managed to keep the country free of the English ascendancy of Henry VIII. As Martin Luther's Protestant teachings started the reformation of the Catholic Church in Germany, then King Henry VIII's England endorsed the new faith, and then the Netherlands, Beaton fought to keep the true Catholic faith and keep out the spread of Protestants within the Scottish borders. With his uncle's direction and strong stance against Protestants, which had been shown by the public burning of the preacher Patrick Hamilton, it was once muttered in advice to Beaton, "If ye burn them, let them burn in low cellars, for the reek of Mister Patrick Hamilton has infected as many as his ashes blew upon."

Not heeding this warning, Beaton would eventually have a public burning of a Protestant preacher outside in the public domain for all to see, right outside his castle in St Andrews. When charged with heresy, the preacher's last words and indeed his ashes would spread the whispers of dissent, creating for David Beaton his own doom! Never had a truer statement been made as a portent of what would happen!

It has to be said that Beaton was a very important figure in the history of St Andrews, and a much travelled man in the duties of his country, serving two monarchs, James V and Mary Queen of Scots. He was born in 1494, to John Beaton of Balfour in Fife and Isobel Moneypenny of Pitmilly.

He was educated in St Andrews, then at the age of seventeen he went to Glasgow University where his uncle James Beaton was archbishop at the time. His name appears in the list of students there in 1511.

Then came the turmoil of the disaster of Flodden field where James IV King of Scotland's proud army was fought to a stalemate in 1513. The two armies, after terrible fighting all day, broke away for the night. Both armies had suffered terrible casualties. But with the news of the missing and dead came the most grievous knowledge that the king's own battalion, which he had been commanding, had been shredded to a man.

War was instigated after a plea from the French queen for aid as they were attacked by England. The French queen sent her own ring in a handkerchief and reminded James of the union between Scotland and France. James went over the border with an army of 20,000 men to meet the might of England and take some pressure off the French.

Now the king and most of his nobles lay dead on the field! Although the English left wing had been beaten and chased from the battle, the Scottish centre had been surrounded and attrition in numbers and superior weaponry had seen the men fall. The Scots footsoldiers had been equipped and armed with 3.5-metre-long wooden pikes with steel spikes, which in close combat were as good as useless. The English foot were armed with the billhook, a wooden-handled, axe-like weapon, and they found it most useful in the confined space of the battle, and put it to much better measure. With the Scottish king and his nobles lying dead on Flodden field, an English invasion of Scotland now seemed imminent!

With news of the disaster and the large number of high-ranking casualties who had fallen with the king, fear soon spread. Never on the field of battle where the St Andrews flag had been proudly held had there been such a calamity. Nearly every noble family had a family member dead on the battlefield. The remains of the Scottish army came in good order to Edinburgh where they set about strengthening the city's walls against the expected English attack and prepared to repel a siege. And as with most noble families in Scotland, the Beatons knew that the very least England would want from them would be hostages to take to England, to be kept as assurance of Scotland's peace.

In 1496 the Scottish education act had ordained that "all Barons and freeholders that are of substance put their eldest sons and heirs to the schools for 8 or 9 years of age and remain at grammar schools till they be competent in Latin – to remain three years at the schools of art". If the English wanted the nobles' firstborn, it would be the schools they would find them at.

With the horrible prospect of the eldest son of the senior noble families being kept in an English castle for endless years – basically in a prison – to keep the peace, young men were speedily sent to Scotland's ally France to escape the English and the prospect of jail.

In fact the expected English attack did not materialise. But David Beaton ended up in Paris, where he amongst other Scots befriended a young James V, who recognised his educated manner and learning and soon struck up a great friendship; he made him his resident speaker at the royal court in Paris. Beaton returned from Paris in 1525 and took his seat in the Scottish Parliament as Abbot of Arbroath. But with trouble brewing again with England in 1533, he was sent as a dignitary with Sir Thomas Erskine in order to renew the Auld Alliance with France and negotiate the marriage of James V with Madeleine, the daughter of the French king, Francis I.

Beaton was a guest at the wedding of the royal pair at Notre-Dame Cathedral in 1537 and then returned with them to Scotland. But disaster struck almost immediately as the young queen took ill with consumption and died two months later.

Beaton was also sent as envoy to King Henry VIII's court, as some difficulty arose between the two kings about Henry's breakaway from the church of Rome. Dialogue was resumed between them, so trusted by James V had he become. Next he was in Paris again, this time to arrange King James' second marriage to Mary of Guise and then escort her back to St Andrews Castle. He then assisted in the coronation of James and Mary. In appreciation of his tasks between the two nations, the kings of Scotland and

France petitioned the Pope to advance him to Cardinal status in 1538, which was granted.

The English king, Henry VIII, again pressed for Scotland to detach itself from its allegiance to the Holy See of Rome as he had done, and to bring the country under his subjection. The Scottish nobles were divided: the powerful Douglas family and some other Scottish nobles supported King Henry's proposal, but with Cardinal Beaton's staunch counsel King James refused Henry's proposal.

Two successive embassies were then sent by Henry VIII to try to change King James' mind, but Beaton sent them homewards, he remained unchanged from his Catholic stance and stayed loyal to Pope Paul III. King Henry was furious from the lack of settlement and the stubbornness of the Scots. War soon broke out, in 1542.

In August a force of 3,000 English men-at-arms invaded Scotland under Sir Robert Bower to assault the Scottish Lowlands. He was met by the Scots lord the Earl of Huntly with 2,000 men at Hadden Rig, where they fought. The English army was attacked and smashed, leaving 800 dead on the Scottish pikes. Hundreds were now prisoners in Scottish hands. But this was only a small ill for King Henry, and he returned with an army the next year, when a force of 2,000 men-at-arms and 500 light horse surprised a Scots force under the Scots Warden Lord Maxwell. It was never much of a battle, some historians saying seven men in total were killed. But the Scots were surprised and caught in a bog where it was impossible to fight, so they panicked and fled the field leaving many of the leaders captive. What had been cleverly planned as a raid into England had ended in disaster. King James V became unwell after the news of the disaster, suffering now from dysentery or cholera. He retired to Falkland Palace and on the 14th December, only 30 years old, he died. Just a week previous to this, his only daughter had been born in Linlithgow: Mary Queen of Scots.

Beaton managed to unite Scotland's unsettled lords into one way of thinking at the next sitting of Parliament at St Andrews. The question was of defence and the national importance of the menace from England and safeguarding the infant queen.

But King Henry VIII had his own plans. He wanted the Scots to renounce the alliance with France, and also wanted his son Prince Edward, who was five, to marry Queen Mary. More envoys appeared to enhance the project. One group contained a Scottish scholar called George Wishart, a Protestant bringing the news from Henry that in years to come any sons from the marriage of the two infants would unite the two kingdoms.

Cardinal Beaton was appointed chancellor of Scotland by the lords of Parliament and continued the resistance to King Henry. He sent back to England his envoys with a staunch refusal of the proposal of a royal marriage. Henry's reaction was to send an army of 16,000 into Scotland and show his displeasure. They burnt down Melrose Abbey, and Dryburgh, Jedburgh and Kelso Abbeys. Retribution from Scotland was swift. When the raiders were caught at Ancrum Moor on the 27th Feb 1545 by the Earl of Angus. The English army was surprised and slaughtered, killing the two leaders Eure and Layton.

With the destruction of the Scottish abbeys, and the fight against the rising tide of Protestantism and Henry

VIII's supporters, Cardinal Beaton was now as important a figure as ever was in St Andrews.

The cardinal's mood was unrelenting and to find a Protestant now inside the Scottish border openly preaching was too much! Drastic measures had to be taken.

It was found that this preacher had found a sympathetic audience. He was a man Beaton had already met in person: he was called George Wishart!

Chapter 4

The Burning of George Wishart

George Wishart was born in 1513, the son of James Wyschart and Elizabeth Learmont. His father was the Laird of Pitarrow.

He studied at Aberdeen University, then eventually started teaching on his own – the New Testament in Greek.

His teachings in a Catholic country brought a charge of heresy from the Bishop of Brechin but he managed to flee to Switzerland, then Germany, becoming passionate towards the Protestant movement on the Continent with the teachings of Martin Luther and Jean Calvin.

He made his way to Henry VIII's Protestant England where he found a position teaching at Corpus Christi College in Cambridge in 1543. In 1544 he was involved as an envoy from King Henry sent with others to push through the marriage of Henry's son Edward to the infant Queen Mary of Scotland. The proposal was bluntly rejected by the Scottish Parliament headed by Cardinal Beaton.

It appears he left Cambrige for good to come home to Scotland, preaching in Montrose. It wasn't long before spies reported this wayward preacher to Beaton, who sent an assassin, a monk called John Weighton, out to kill him.

One day George Wishart had just finished his sermon when his flock had departed. He was picking up his notes when he realised not everyone had left! Standing in front of him was John Weighton, with a dagger in his hand! Wishart threw himself at his attacker; he fought the man and managed to take the dagger off him. The man fell to the floor in tears, and on his knees confessed all. The townsfolk demanded that Wishart deliver the traitor to them or they would take him by force, and they burst in with intention of lynching the assassin. George Wishart held the man captive in his arms declaring, "Whoever hurts him shall hurt me, for he has done me no mischief but much good, by teaching more heedfulness for time to come." The townsfolk were very impressed that George Wishart had saved the life of his attacker. The whole plan had backfired for Cardinal Beaton, for the priest had confessed. A grumbling of discontent now grew in Montrose against the wayward cardinal.

Another attempt was made shortly after by the Cardinal. A forged letter was sent to Wishart, supposedly from his friend the Laird of Kinnear who asked him with speed to come to him as he was gravely sick! It was a trap – the cardinal had set sixty armed men in hiding, to ambush Wishart and murder him.

The letter was delivered by a boy, who also had a horse for the journey for Wishart. Something wasn't right! Wishart was uneasy about the offer of a horse, he was suspicious about the plea. To make sure, he made some of his friends go in his place instead. The trap was discovered and they made their way back quickly, to reveal the intended plan. Wishart declared, "I was assured there was treason. I know I shall end my life by that bloodthirsty man's hands but it will not be in this manner."

In fear of his safety in Montrose, Wishart moved to Edinburgh. He resided with an old friend, Mr Cockburn (of Ormiston in East Lothian). But the cardinal's spies were everywhere, and he had been seen!

The place was surrounded by the Earl of Bothwell's men and against protest from Mr Cockburn, George Wishart was arrested and dragged from the house to Edinburgh Castle. Here he was collected by Beaton's men and transported to the castle of St Andrews. The dreaded bottle dungeon awaited him.

The trial was swift and one-sided. He was asked to recant his Protestant teachings. His composure under this heavy threat was remarkable and praiseworthy, but in his heart Wishart knew he was a doomed man! He was too firmly fixed in his religious principles to change his Protestant stance! A charge of heresy was declared and he was condemned to burn at the stake, right outside St Andrews Castle, where Beaton could watch at his pleasure.

What a miserable end awaited Wishart! He waited in the filth of the dungeon as his stake was fitted, and wood and tar were collected for his burning.

Above in the castle, Cardinal Beaton was turning the event into a showpiece. Red cushions were placed on the castle walls for the abbots to sit in comfort and view the spectacle; food was ordered; kitchens were busy preparing roasts and fine wines. It was to be a big turnout for a very special occasion, and full of pomp. No expense was spared. Finally Beaton would wipe the smile from the face of this traitorous Scottish ambassador who brought King Henry VIII's claims in person. The man had the audacity to venture back into his homeland and preach the words of Martin Luther's heretical Protestant movement! Wishart had been a problem to Beaton, and his failed assassins had brought nothing but wicked whispers against him. An example had to be set, the way his uncle had done with Patrick Hamilton.

What George Wishart's thoughts were at that moment are not recorded, but a verse from 1890 by D. A. Kilroune found in a book called the *Handbook to Fife* records in poetic form a fine view of this wretched soul in the bottle dungeon at that time ...

> Down – down – down!
>   With chain and windless and cord;
> For no step is hewn for foot of man,
>   Into that deep gulf abhorred.
> No voice from upper world
>   And no change of night or day
> No record to mark the dreary hours
>   As they slowly pass away
> What a thought of what is nigh
>   What each slow hour brings nigher
> The chain, the stake, the gazing crowd
>   The grim and torturing fire!

The 1st of March 1546. The stake was fixed, wood piled and ready, tar barrel set ... all was ready as the deacons and abbots took their places on the cushions on the castle walls, helping themselves to meats and pastries and fine wines, as down below the castle the crowds grew for the occasion. Beaton sat at his bedroom window at the castle, thus having the best seat for viewing the approaching entertainment.

Only 33 years of age, tall and handsome, Wishart was brought from the bottle-dungeon. As two friars put a black linen coat on him, another packed several hidden bags of gunpowder around his body, in an act of kindness. This was to bring about his death quickly before the flames. He was brought out in front of the castle and tied to the stake, the crowd silent. The fire was started.

He cried out a last few words: "This fire torments my body, but no wise abates my spirit." He looked towards the castle and its spectators. "He who in

The Martyrs' Monument commemorating George Wishart and others

such state, from that high place, feedeth his eyes with my torments shall be hanged out these windows to be seen with as such ignominy as he leaneth there in pride now!"

The executioner began to strangle George Wishart with a knotted cord as the flames took light. The bishops and cardinal sat in luxury enjoying the spectacle as God's work was done before them, eating grapes and rejoicing. The smoke billowed and a strong north-east wind started up. St Andrews is used to buffeting winds, but at that same moment the gunpowder belts around Wishart blew all at once in a mighty explosion. Whether it was the sudden approaching storm or the blast of the gunpowder, several figures fell into the sea from the castle battlements, to drown in the full tide below.

It was an ill omen for things to come, as Wishart's carcass burned away for the next three hours and the crowd, covered in the ashes of a true martyr, ventured back to their homes with voices of dissent.

Wishart's supporters were up in arms in a calculated revenge only two months later.

Norman Lesley, master of Rothes, was one of the victorious leaders at the battle of Ancrum Moor in 1545 against the English. Now he came forward with a grievance over land disputes against the cardinal, and led the rebellion together with his brother John, who swore that his dagger in his hand should be thrust into the cardinal's heart. With the Lesleys came the Kirkcaldys of Grange, who were redoubtable soldiers, James Melville and other Fife lairds.

On the 28th May, these men, in a party of fifteen, dressed as tradesmen in capes and hoods, attracted no attention as they walked amongst the builders strengthening the castle walls. Masons, stonewrights and carpenters went about their business as they mingled among them to enter the castle gate.

Over a hundred masons were at work, and Beaton was in the middle of constructing a new round tower or block house. Beaton had fifty retainers and soldiers present in the castle. He was a man accustomed to stratagems and security, so the ease with which these fifteen assassins penetrated the castle is very peculiar indeed.

The captain of the garrison was great friends with Wishart, offering him a breakfast on the day of his martyrdom. According to John Knox, a plot within the castle walls helped the "fifteen" enter so easily.

Early in the morning the "fifteen", among the daily tradesmen, casually walked through the portcullis gate where the drawbridge was down. Kirkcaldy of Grange engaged the porter in small talk as the others followed; the porter saw swords under the disguise and tried to raise the alarm for his master asleep upstairs. He was dirked and thrown into the moat!

Shouts went up, as all the tradesmen ran for the exits, and the assassins sought their quarry. From his window in his nightgown the cardinal saw the slain porter and realised his castle was taken. Beaton retreated into his bedchamber and barricaded the door. He had his two-handed sword in the room, and a chamberlain with him. When the door was forced, he was found seated in his chair calling for leniency, because he was a priest!

None was given, and John Lesley and Peter Carmichael hacked him to the ground with claymore swords, John Melville giving the fatal blow with a dirk! ... The cardinal was dead!

Those loyal to the cardinal in St Andrews now raised their swords and came running. Around four hundred were outside the castle, whose drawbridge was down, per-mitting entry. "What have you done to the Lord Cardinal?" they cried. "Have you slain him? Let us see him!" ... And see him they did, as his body was hung out the window, the very window where not two months before Beaton had sat and relaxed as Wishart burned and uttered his oaths. An arm and a foot were hung out for the crowd to see that he was indeed slain.

The Master of Rothes shouted to the hordes, "There is your God and now be satisfied – get you home to your houses."

Beaton's body was salted, wrapped in a sheet of lead and thrown into the bottle dungeon where countless others had been thrown before by the cardinal's order.

*

The castle was taken, and with the news more Fife lairds joined the rebels inside the castle: Henry Balnevis (who was long in King Henry's pay), the family of Learmont, the Moneypennys of Pitmillie, a priest John Rough and another preacher called John Knox, a follower of George Wishart who was already being chased by Beaton's spies. In all over 150 men were now in command of the castle.

News of the cardinal's death delighted King Henry, but in France a fleet of warships was sent to aid the infant Queen Mary's forces.

The Earl of Arran, whose son was a guest of Beaton and was now prisoner in the castle, took command of the Scottish forces and besieged the castle in the name of Queen Mary. Trenches were dug, cannons brought forward and the castle was pounded.

The castle defenders fought bravely, the two heavy guns brought up to devastate the walls lost all their gunners to arrows and small cannon from the walls of the keep. The defenders were declared traitors, but it mattered naught as they fought to keep the Protestant flag flying. They expected rescue from England and her Protestant king.

At the time of the stalemate, a network of tunnels was dug to undermine the keep, set charges and blow the rebels out! The south-east corner of the castle was the start of the first one, a passage about two metres wide and just over two metres high extending 25 metres, running to the tower. All constructed through thick sandstone, the effort in the construction of this tunnel was of immense scale and dangerously done under fire from the defenders. At length they had the distance and the tunnel extended right under the tower, ready to be stuffed full of gunpowder and blow the castle open in a mighty explosion.

But unknown to the Earl of Arran's forces the castle rebels had dug a secondary mine, right above the one now finished! The two forces broke through to each other and hand-to-hand fighting in the tunnels now commenced.

A fleet of ships was seen on the horizon and at last after ten months it looked like the English had come to the aid of the defenders, but with cannons primed they fired upon the castle. It wasn't the English — it was the French. The castle was attacked in force by sea. Now a small-bore cannon was raised to the top of St Rule's Tower by ropes and was positioned looking down into the castle. It's a wonder the Earl of Arran never thought of this action earlier, but then again his son was a captive inside. Now the castle could be pounded with cannonfire directed at the inner walls. With the combined firepower from sea and land, the south castle wall was struck and badly damaged, and so in a short while collapsed into ruins, with many of the defenders on this wall killed. The castle was taken, and the brave rebels surrendered to the French. It had taken a whole year to breech the castle.

The prisoners were taken on board, a hundred and twenty of them, and treated as galley slaves. A great booty in silver, clothes and armour was taken by the French. The prisoners were chained to oars in the bowels of the ships and made to row them.

Beaton's body was still in the bottle dungeon, it had lain there since the start of the battle a year ago. Pickled in a barrel of vinegar, it was then wrapped in a lead sheet and buried in the Blackfriars church. No one knows the exact spot. The cardinal's tragedy had finished but the Protestant Reformation had only started!

Chapter 5

Two Men with a Destiny of Witchcraft

Two of the castle defenders, John Knox and James Melville, now found themselves with the others on board a French galley; they would row in the discomfort of cold and hellish seas for the next three years, not being freed until the winter of 1549. But as partners in the castle rebellion their bond was strong, and it would be back home in St Andrews where they made their names in history and witchcraft.

In the three years John Knox and James Melville had been galley slaves, back in St Andrews another cardinal called Archbishop Hamilton had taken control. He once again was repairing the destroyed castle and yet again another heretic had been accosted and burned in St Andrews. Walter Milne was an 82-year-old priest from Angus; he was sentenced as a heretic, again in the same circumstances as George Wishart, but this time no citizen of St Andrews was prepared to sell rope or timbers to the Church to do the deed. He was eventually burned on the clifftop next to the castle. Public opinion was for the Reformation. George Wishart's teachings and his terrible end had transformed many people's thoughts about why they put up with this brutal regime of churchmen sitting in the comfort of cathedrals and castles, paying no taxes, dictating all and having the say over life or death for those who questioned them! All they needed was a leader, someone sitting as a galley slave perhaps?

Once released by the French, Knox and Melville weren't in too bad health; Knox had actually been able to write a book aboard his galley ship. They made their way back to Scotland and St Andrews, and started preaching again. This time the sermons were packed and enough people were there to defy Archbishop Hamilton and his fellow deacons openly.

Knox had been a friend of George Wishart and a disciple of his teachings. With three years to ponder in a French galley, he resurfaced in St Andrews full of vengeance. Now he had his pulpit, and attacked the Catholics from within their own churches. He cried, "Pull down the doocots and the doos will flee." With this the Catholic houses of religion were attacked by Protestant mobs and wrecked. His hatred of the Catholics with their treasures and holy idols hit home; the anti-Roman feelings were strong for a rebellion in the city. They marched towards the cathedral, hundreds in number, and forced entry with Archbishop Hamilton and his priests inside. The doors gave way and they smashed the place from within. The devastation spread to the other churches in St Andrews – some were burnt down. Every element of Popishness and idolatry was destroyed and the priors chased out of St Andrews. Other monasteries in Scotland would follow suit.

Before Knox's sermons Archbishop Hamilton had an abundance of clergy, forty chaplains, a priory of thirty-four canons, a provost and twelve prebendaries, and a Dominican and Franciscan monastery, also a teaching clergy in three colleges. Within a month all was destroyed, relics were stolen or destroyed and the priests gone ... so quick and absolute was the chaos. But the most precious relic of all was held in the box made out of King Edward of England's gold and diamonds. The bones of St Andrew were taken and hidden, or maybe smashed and lost forever!

The haunting remains of the cathedral destroyed after John Knox's sermon

It seems the violence from John Knox's speech spread fast, with the monastery the centre of their fury. It seems incredible that such an important relic as the armbone of St Andrew was lost to the world. It was so valuable in itself and stood for the very city it dedicated its name to. For this rich item to have gone missing it is more probable that it was hurriedly buried by the monks or locked away in a secret place and that those who knew the secret were killed. Many writers claim it was destroyed by the mob, but I suggest such a precious item would be the first thing the monks reached to save!

Today the cathedral is a glorious ruin and one can look and wonder at the majesty of the place when it was fully built. Historians state that the wreckage of the building was due not to John Knox's followers but to the neglect of an absent owner. With the monks chased away and building works uncompleted it wasn't long till the elements brought the roof down. After that it was a free-for-all as the majestic ruin became a quarry for the nearby housing projects.

With the clergy chased from St Andrews, John Knox took over, introducing Protestant sympathisers as parish ministers. The flames of Protestantism spread over lower Scotland.

James Melville filled the vacant position at St Mary's College. From here with his growing family he moved to the larger parish at Kilrenny and in Anstruther he built a splendid house, a few hours' ride to St Andrews if he was called over by his friend John Knox.

In 1569 the first of a series of witch hunts took place in St Andrews. Mary Queen of Scots in her ninth parliament endorsed the Witchcraft Act in 1563, six months after her

James Melville's manse

cousin Queen Elizabeth of England did the same. It was now a capital crime. "Witch" was a term mentioned in the pages of the Bible, (Exodus 22.18 "thou shalt not suffer a witch to live"). It was taken to new heights with Pope Innocent VIII's papal bull where two German friars wrote a book on how to find a witch, search her and destroy her. To justify their methods they used "information" such as: "woman was made from Adam's rib in Eden, the rib is bent so therefore are women and they waver in their faiths, they vindicate themselves with the act of witchcraft".

Their book called *Malleus Maleficarum* was written and published showing the grotesque methods of torturing a witch to gain a confession. Once the witch had confessed to whatever ills she was meant to have done, a further confession was undertaken but without torture and punishments, hence a "free" confession. Once this was obtained, the witch was ready to go to the next stage in the book ... termination!

Once burnt at the stake, as were all heretics, the property of the witch such as boats or farms were incorporated into the church funds ... a brilliant method of ridding itself of potential enemies and boosting the Church's flocks by the simple superstitious method of fear!

The first witch found in St Andrews was in 1569, called Nic Neville, who in the sketchy details we have on him was "condamnit to the death and brynt". In the same year another called William Stewart was executed "for dyvers points of witchcraft and necromancie". This was under Archbishop John Hamilton who would live one year more before being arrested on the charge of burning the martyr Walter Miln unlawfully ... he was hanged in Stirling in 1570.

1572 ... April 28th ... A woman burnt as a witch ... witnessed by James Melville and condemned from the pulpit by John Knox. "She being set up at a pillar before him" ... No details exist of her name.

1575 ... January 18–25 ... Marjorye Smyth dilatit (denounced) and accused of witchcraft ... both Marjorye and her husband flew the city before capture.

1581 ... October 26 ... Bessy Robertson delatit for witchcraft ... (Unclear what the end result was ... no verdict)

1588 ... Alison Peirson of Byrehill ... Dilated on various points of witchcraft ...

In 1588 the Archbishop was Patrick Adamson who was created by James VI. At this time he was going through a great deal of discomfort with personal health problems, doctors could find no remedy for his problem and praying for himself to get better did no favours. James Melville brought his brother's daughter Agnes Melville, a woman gifted in herbs and medicines, to treat the ill archbishop, but her skills were wasted as Patrick Adamson got worse.

Then there appeared another healer from the Boarhills who continued after Agnes Melville's work seemed to have failed. Alison Pierson, this highly-rated healer, immediately set her medicines to good use, feeding him a stewed fowl and two draughts of claret laced with the drugs she recommended. His condition was said to be dropsy, a condition that leaves the body swollen with water retention (oedema). The medicines took a few weeks to work but the archbishop recovered completely. His gratitude towards Alison and her miraculous work was shown after she asked for some coin in payment!

She is next on record "transferring the archbishop's indisposition from himself to a white palfrey, which died in consequence". She was accused of being a necromancer and witch by the archbishop. She was burnt in St Andrews in

1588, not long after her trial. With the suspicion that witchcraft had been used to treat the archbishop, the finger of blame now pointed at Agnes Melville who was first to help the ill man. In the parish records it states...

1588 ... July 17 ... Agness Melville daughter to umquhill (deceased) Andro Melville elder to Kirk in Anstruther ... being delatit as ane suspect of witchcraft ...

The accusation was pressed no further in the court records, her uncle James Melville probably using his considerable position to save his niece. But the stigma of being accused as a witch doesn't go away easily, as we shall see.

With the death of Agnes's uncle James Melville around 1592, her shield against accusations was gone. In the parish records the new minister of Pittenweem, Nicol Dalgleish, had collected witches from Pittenweem and Largo including one called Agness Melville and deposited them into the bottle-dungeon of the castle, all awaiting trial for witchcraft.

1595 ... September 10 ... "Several persons decernit (decreed) to mak public humiliation for fetching of Agnes Melville, ane condamnit witch and two other witches".

Elspet Gilchrist and Jonet Lochequoir were burnt with Agness Melville.

1613 ... September ... Agnes Anstruther suspect of witchcraft.

1614 ... Agnes Anstruther and Isobell Jhonestowne to be proceeded against for witchcraft. (Both found guilty, Agness spent nearly a year in the bottle-dungeon)

1630 ... Commission to the bailie of the regality of St Andrews for the putting of Margaret Callender to the trial of an assize for witchcraft.

1644 ... Bessie Mason ... mentioned as "umquhil (dead, sentence has been carried out) a confessing witch."

1660 ... April 12th ... Catherine Fraser was brought before the Kirk session of St Andrews for cursing Alexander Duncan and his horse. His horse took ill and died in a short space of time.

1667 ... Commission for trial of Issobel Key, prisoner in the tolbooth guilty of witchcraft ... (having a guilty verdict could only lead to the stake for this woman, but it seems the Tolbooth jail was now preferred as the jail to the bottle-dungeon, or it was already too full!) For a while she lived with the daughter of Lundy Mill.

John Knox from his church in St Andrews became the leading figure in the Protestant Reformation, gaining enough power to publicly chastise the Scottish Queen Mary for her stance as a Catholic. But he himself when in old age took a younger wife, and his enemies presumed witchcraft had been used. He was called "an auld decrepit creature of maist base degree" in wooing Margaret Stewart, the young daughter of Andrew Stewart. It was thought Knox had had diabolical aid to procure this young woman, he being over fifty years old and the girl a beautiful virgin of seventeen. He was accused of "raising some sancts (spirits) in his own yard, among them the devil with horns" which is supposed to have driven Knox's servant Richard Bannatyne to a madness from which he never recovered, and died.

The case against Knox became nothing but wicked rumour and luckily never reached the heights of court. The marriage went ahead in 1564 and would produce three daughters, Martha, Margaret and Elizabeth. John Knox would live till 1572 when at the age of 59 he died. He has a burial plot in Edinburgh at St Giles Cathedral in Edinburgh.

I did find one more accused witch with a connection to St Andrews and again it is a very sad tale, somewhat pitiful

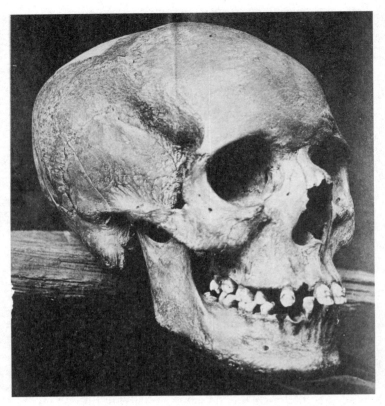

in what was later found out from modern-day doctors about the woman. Lilias Adie was from Torryburn, a coastal village near Dunfermline. She was accused of witchcraft in 1705, taken to the jail there and tortured. They were hard on the woman and alas she died during the parish's efforts to extract a confession. But once she was dead, the parish had a dilemma! What to do with her body? They couldn't bury her as she was still a suspected witch! And they couldn't burn her as she had never confessed! The problem was solved when they decided to bury her at the high tide mark of the beach. And there her body lay for the

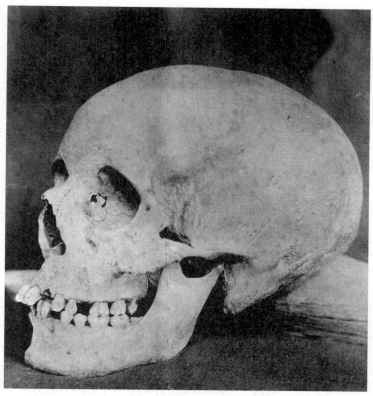

In 1874 Dr William Dow photographed the skull
of Lilias Adie (*National Library of Scotland*)

next eighty years, until a damask weaver and designer,
Joseph Neil Paton, put her bones on display in his
collection of curiosities. (His son Sir Noel Paton became a
favourite of Queen Victoria, who commissioned some
paintings from him.) When he died (1874) his collection
was auctioned. In 1884 a Dumfermline doctor took Lilias'
bones to St Andrews University where he studied the skull,
noting "it was very small in size, a diseased brain, probably
mongoloid". His description of the skull gives us some

63

Spoon and a Key, *from St. Serf's Island, Loch Leven*
730 A Mummy Hand, Piece of the Crieff Gallows, and Sundry other Relics
731 Lot of Old Keys, &c.
732 Lot of Brass Book and Drawer Mountings
733 Skull, with other Bones, and portion of the Coffin of Lilias Adie, who, on her own confession, was condemned to be burnt for witchcraft at Torrieburn, but died under torture in the bell-tower of the church, while preparations were in progress for her execution. She was buried within the seamark near Torrieburn, where these relics were obtained on the opening of her grave about 35 years ago
734 Skull of Jenny Nettle, celebrated in Scottish Song
735 A Number of Plaster Casts of Heads of Noted

Auction catalogue – Lilias Adie's skull was auctioned in 1874

possible reasons why Lilias Adie stood out as unusual from others and was accused of being a witch.

In my last book *Largo's Untold Stories* I had information on two facial reconstructions, one a Pictish woman and the other an Arctic explorer who was cannibalised. I am in the process of tracking the skull down; it hasn't been seen for a hundred years but may lie somewhere in the archives of St Andrews Museum. One day I shall find Lilias and have her face reconstructed like the ones in my book.

My first book *The Weem Witch* covered the story of the 28 witches found in Pittenweem – six of them were burnt in St Andrews. I campaigned to deaf ears for a monument to Pittenweem's murdered citizens. Many complained about "the waste of money" for my cause, while in St Andrews a fund of £145,000 was soon raised to smarten up the Martyrs' Monument. Once again religion gets preference over the plebs of its witch hunts, and the ministers get heroic idols to cherish their memory, while the slain murdered small folk get nothing but disdain ... Is it time for another reformation?

Chapter 6

Fornicators, Fornicating Fornicators!

Law in St Andrews came via the ministers as well as the civil courts. The St Andrews Kirk Session met weekly to judge offences from minor discrepancies to heinous crimes!

Today we may laugh at the records held within the Kirk Session register, where the consequences of not turning up in church on a Sunday or a quick fumble with an unmarried woman beneath the sheets brought the wrath of the Kirk down on you. But it could dish out the most severe of punishments.

Many of the cases heard are given the term "ward" or "warding" which was applied to the accused as a confinement, whether in his own house, private lodgings or the town jail or Tolbooth. The offender was often kept confined till a fine was paid or his time was done.

After the proscription of "Popery" by Parliament in 1560, the crime of fornication was outlawed and the kirks took a hard stance. The dictionary definition of fornication as "to commit sexual intercourse without being married, to have sex with an unmarried person, adultery". But in the Scotland of 1563 it was turned into a capital crime by Queen Mary's parliament:

"It is statute and ordained that all notour and manifest commiters of adulterie in onie time to cum shall be punished with all rigour unto the deid, as well the woman as the man."

St Andrews took a hard stance on the fornicators. If when summoned by the Kirk you failed to appear at church court, the sheriff and his men came in force to find you! However there is no evidence of a man or woman being executed for the crime of fornication in St Andrews, although in other parts of Scotland there are records of people who were executed for such crimes.

In 1559 a man charged with "the filthy crime of adultery has been keepit in ward in the tolbooth for sixteen weeks"!

And John Guthrie, a notorious adulterer before the Kirk Session of Kirkliston in 1617 did penance in sack-cloth for his impurities, and was later hanged!

The Kirk Session courts in Scotland had a system of penalties:−

First offence ... fined forty pounds Scots ... failure to pay meant eight days in prison on a diet of bread and water and two hours in the stocks, where all manner of filth would be thrown at you by the locals.

Second offence ... fined a hundred merks (about 67 pounds Scots) and your head shaven and made to wear a sack as clothes, plus time in the stocks!

Third offence ... fined a hundred pounds Scots, and three times on the ducking stool, then banished from the town forever.

To be banished was to be thrown out of town, and hopefully another parish would take pity and take you inside its borders. Basically the original parish was no longer inconvenienced with you, but a treacherous unprotected life among the turnpikes while finding another place to stay −

that brought its own dangers, set among the dregs of society, being villains, thieves and cut-throats.

For lesser crimes, as we shall see, the stool of repentance (the cutty stool) was used in church, where the guilty would be embarrassed by public humiliation in front of the church congregation – forced to kneel on the stool and have a minister shout at you as you admitted your crime. Other crimes could see the guilty stripped naked and forced to wear a sack of hemp for modesty, sometimes being made to walk through the town from one gate to the other while being whipped by the guards, and usually having a board around your neck declaring your offences.

In the villages a "thief's hole" or secure room would be used to lock up drunks and sabbath breakers, but without a permanent guard, jail breaks were not uncommon. Iron chains with a collar and padlock for the neck were found in many of the church grounds. Fixed to a wall with a small chain, the "jougs" never gave the participant a chance to sit and rest, being forced by the shortness of the chain to stand.

In histories of St Andrews many authors mention the "witch pool" which was a ducking pool below today's Martyrs Monument at the bottom of the witch hill. It was never used for witches, despite its name. Scotland never drowned witches as her English neighbours did. There are plenty of poems and songs in Scottish literature mentioning the ducking of witches – David Vader's 19th-century poem about the Pittenweem witch being "ducked in Kilconquer Loch" is one – but it's all artistic licence. No evidence exists of any such act. The Pittenweem witch Janet Cornfoot, as recounted in my book *The Weem Witch*, was hung by a ship's mast and cast into the sea in a ducking manner, but this was mob action, not official policy.

What is known of the ducking pool in St Andrews and the activities carried out there are briefly mentioned in Robert Chambers' *Domestic Annals of Scotland* (1859) where it is recorded that the Scottish Regent in 1568, Regent Moray, once "rode to St Andrews and causit a man to drown callit Alexander Macker and six more men for piracy using the 'witches pool'."

It was important to the church to see sinners disgraced properly. Some ministers were more lenient than others, as we shall see when the ministers Wallace and Black take charge of the Sessions in St Andrews. But their harsh stance would carry a cost when King James VI came to remove them in person when they went too far. The public was the eyes and ears of the Kirk Session, with many very eager to testify against sinners, and make themselves look good in the eyes of the ministry. Swearing and all manner of cursing were frowned upon, and severe penalties were delivered. The next few pages come straight from the Parish Session registers in St Andrews 1559–1582. I have taken the liberty of shortening the entries and softening the harsh Scots language to make it easier reading for today's reader, but also for the cases not to become repetitive.

There is case upon case upon case of fornication. It really was pandemic at times, and if I wrote up every case of fornication it would become so repetitive the reader might begin to tire. Needless to say, I have dug through the records to give you the most interesting cases. I have added some comments to help. It really is fascinating to see how our ancestors still couldn't keep their hands off each other – even though they knew the consequences if and when caught!

ST ANDREWS KIRK SESSIONS 1559–1582

March 1559 ... the quhilk day (on which day) Andro Lummisden called for nocht adhering to Besse Smyth his spows. He confesses that he hais nocht adheyred to her in bed this twelf yeir bigane. In respect of his confessioun, and delatioun past thereupon, the ministers and eldaris decerness (orders) him to adheyre in bed and buyrd (board), within fourty aucht houris (forty-eight hours), to.his said spows; and to lat the samyne adheyreing be notified to the minister and eldaris forsaid, within aucht daiis (eight days) efter ... under the payne of all severe ecclesiasticall discipline ...

[Dear oh dear! Andrew Lumsden called for not "adhering" to his wife! In an age of large families, a women when married expected children. Whether it was she herself or another member of the family, someone has complained to the Church about her lack of action beneath the bedsheets and now husband Andrew has been ordered to perform "within 48 hours" and then let the Parish know! The Kirk Session for December above is how it was written in the records, the dialect takes a bit getting used to. In the following Kirk Session records I have softened the old Scots dialect into a more readable text.]

April 1560 ... On this day Mr John Todrick and Margaret Ramsay being called for the crime of adultery before the minister, elders and council, to do penance for the said sin, and finding no penance in them are suspended for further trying of their sin. To the effect that signs of worthy repentance may be spurred on them with prayers and common supplications from the congregation.

April 1560 ... Catherine Tweddell claimed that by the seduction of Walter Ramsey, a man living in this city, "I have given my body to be used by him where now I have conceived and born a bairn to him, and all this I have done because in the presence of God only he gave me his faith that he should fulfil the bond of marriage in face of the congregation or Holy Kirk, which promise he renewed to me, by giving me his right hand before I would consent to his desires; and now the said Walter denies the said faithful promise of marriage made to me. I seek your wisdoms here to cause and compel him to fulfil that which he made, a faithful promise of marriage to me here, according to the law of God."

The Council, Ministers and Elders according to the law of God order the said Walter to complete the said bond with the said Catherine. Because the woman is alleged herself to be a virgin before he got her and he could say nothing contrary to that, time and place being offered to him to object to the contrary and prove the same ...

[All the way through this ledger, many women are making the same complaint about marriage proposals not being fulfilled.]

May 1560 ... Margaret Murdow delated (denounced) for blasphemous sayings against the sacrament of the body and blood of Christ, saying words in the open fish market.

[At this time the Protestant rebellion was at its infancy and any talk of dissent would be curbed.]

May 1560 ... Andrew Howburne and Margaret Downe, fornicators, continued in correction till Thursday the 9th day of May ... marriage to be completed against them.

[For those unable to pay the fine for the crime of fornication, an eight-day jail term followed, then forced marriage.]

May 1560 ... Patrick Ramsey is obliged to take the bairn gotten upon Bessie Small and provide a nurse to the same and the woman obliged to pay 20 shillings yearly till the bairn be seven, and the bairn taken from her betwixt now and Sunday next.

[She's an unfit or ill mother? A wet nurse has been provided for at cost of twenty shillings a year.]

June 1560 ... Right venerable minister and elders unto your wisdoms, David Gudlawd claims that is not unknown that Margaret Archibald my spouse for the time and Christine Petbladow her mother, spouse to umquhile [dead] Andrew Archibald then alive, in 1524 departed furth of this realm, without the knowledge or consent of any of us, their said husbands, being both suspected adulterers, as the council has shown in the said Margaret, by defiling of my bed, taking another party in pretended matrimony for 35 years. In that time I have lived a continent life without any suspicion. And now having respect to my age that I may not be at ease alone and finding Catherine Niesche, a chaste virgin past 40 years of age, have procured her consent to be joined with me in matrimony. Trusting that the said Margaret is deceased ... I beseech your wisdoms to grant me an edict ...

[An honest letter from a man married 35 years and now probably widowed, who wants to marry again.]

1561 ... In the actions and cause of divorce intended by Gelis Scrimgeor against Archebald Dundas, her husband, for the filthy crime of adultery committed by him with Anne Duncan and Catren Cragdenny ... the Superintendent ... finds the adultery confessed by Archebald ... pronounces and, with the advice and council of the ministry, declares the said Archebald an adulterer; and therefore according to the law of God, the said Gelis Scrimgeor separated and divorced from him.

[Archebald was to be committed to the hands of the magistrates to whom he was subject and to undergo civil correction for his crimes.]

April 1561 ... John Gyb in Wester Strathor is convicted before the Superintendent and ministry of St Andrews, at the instance of Margaret Hillok his spouse. Margaret proposes an action of divorce against him and alleges she has been his married wife and companion in board and bed in the space of two years last and mostly obeyed her husband. She claims divorce on grounds he was impotent of nature.

[John, after many an excuse, at length confesses this!]

The Superintendent with advice from the ministry, fearing deceit to be in the matter, instructs John and Margaret to cohere and keep company together and to treat each other as becomes man and wife joined in matrimony for at least three quarters of a year.

March 1562 ... John Gyb appears in court again having been summoned by the Superintendent at the instance of Margaret Hillok to hear the case of divorce alleged by her.

The Superintendent with advice of his council instructs John Gyb and Margaret to cohere and keep mutual cohabitation, and to treat each other in bed and board as becomes lawful husband and wife within 15 days.

1562 ... Taking evidence on the claim of marriage proposed between Margaret Steynson with Andrew Brown parishioners of Largo. The parties summoned ... it is found by confession that Margaret kept as a virgin undeflowered resident in her father's house, Andrew Brown came and pursued and persuaded her to grant and consent to his lust, and she refused to consent, unless he would make her an honest woman. Andrew answered saying, "Is not my father's son good enough for your father's daughter?" and in that instant and pronunciation of those words they joined their hands together, and consequently their bodies. And Andrew, questioned, knows nor alleges anything contrary but that Margaret was a virgin at the first intercourse together.

The Superintendent with advice of the ministry, determines the said Andrew to solemnise marriage with Margaret, within 40 days, according to the law of God and her claim, under pain of excommunication. And concerning the allegation and confession made by Andrew of carnal intercourse had by him with Margaret Alan finds the same a manifest transgression of the law of God and for this commits him to be civilly punished by gentlemen and elders of the parish of Largo.

1562 ... Andrew Olephant and Issobell Mortoun denounced and accused for keeping company in bed and board unmarried, to the offence of God and disgrace of the congregation.

The said Andrew confesses their keeping company as is stated, and alleges they have made promise of marriage and are willing to solemnise their marriage ... and submit to discipline.

The ministry ordains them to appear in the congregation, to make public satisfaction, and then their banns to be proclaimed, and within 21 days to solemnise their marriage.

[21 days gave them three Sundays to declare the banns.]

May 1563 ... Both the said parties summoned on this day to hear pronounced in the said case and Margret appearing, the Superintendent, advised with the process and all therein deduced, finds no case of impotence proven, and therefore absolves John Gyb [our seedless friend again] from the instance of Margret as it is intended, and their marriage to have been and be lawful, and so to remain until some case be alleged and proven.

[It looks like poor John's still not having any luck producing children, to the disgust of his wife, but the Kirk still won't let them divorce.]

July 1563 ... Margret, in penalty of non appearance of John Gyb, alleges that the said John is and has been at all times impotent to her, and also has confessed himself an adulterer in giving of his body to Donis Dorkye, has cut off himself from her, and so she should be divorced, separated and divided from John; and asks the Superintendent so to decide against the said John, and free her to marry with any other lawful husband according to the law of God.

August 1563 ... judgement is given in case of divorce moved by Margret Hyllok against John Gyb for adultery committed by the said John with Donis Dorkye, transgressing the third command of the second table and law of God, where it is written, Thou shall not commit adultery ...

On the 4th of June in the ninth year of Queen Mary Stuart's parliament, a bill was produced to deal with the huge amount of fornication clogging the church courts. The bill, very threatening as it seems, did nothing to stem the flow of fornicators in the courts.

"For as much as the abominable and filthy vice and crime of adultery has been perniciously and wickedly used within this Realm in times bygone, ... It is enacted and ordained, by Queen's Majesty and the Estates in Parliament, that all notorious and manifest committers of adultery, in any time to come after this date [4th June 1563] shall be punished with all rigour unto the death, as well the woman as the man doer and committer of the same, after due warning be made to abstain from the said manifest and notorious crime; and for other adultery, that the acts and laws made thereupon of before be put to execution with all rigour; and also declares that this act in no wise shall prejudge any party to pursue for divorcement for the crimes of adultery before committed conforming to the law."

[To commit adultery now had the maximum penalty as punishment ... Death!]

July 1563 ... Sir David Donaldson was summoned to have appeared before the Superintendent, personally app-rehended, to submit to correction and discipline, regarding the denunciation given in against him as blasphemously speaking against the preached word of God and religion, and also as a whore-monger [ane huyr-mongar], having two different women at that time with bairn to him begotten in whoredom; often called and not appearing, the Superintendent, with advice of the ministry of St Andrews, decrees prohibition to be sent to the minister of Monimail to be executed there, commanding all God fearing Christians to abstain from all society and company of the said Sir David, declaring him to be found and known to be a stubborn Papist, a blasphemous speaker against the truth of God's word, and an obvious hardened whore-monger, unworthy to have society or fellowship with any of the godly, and relation to be made of his vicious life and disobedience to the Justice Clerk.

March 1564 ... Today James Lyell, former Papist priest, confesses himself to have recanted and renounced all Papistry ...

[James had been previously summoned for the slaughter of Cardinal Beaton (amongst others); his change of faith may explain his reason to be involved in the late Cardinal Beaton's death.]

August 1564 ... Today Robert Nycholson and Jonat Efflek his spouse summoned by the Superintendent's letters and appearing, they are charged to adhere as man and wife, or else to give reasonable cause why they should not do so. Robert alleges he should not adhere to Jonat because the said Jonat Efflek as he alleges, has given her body to William Donaldson, married man, dwelling in Stirling, at the Ruid-day [the day of the Invention of the Cross], being at the fair in Kilconquar. Robert being demanded if he would prove his allegation, if he should be admitted to prove the same before the justice, where the said Jonat would suffer death for her offence according to the law, the said Robert – hearing of the danger, moved by pity towards his wife, of his own free will – pardoned her upon this condition, that she shall become obliged to be a true partner and servant to Robert in future; and if at any time after this she be found guilty in giving her body to any person but her husband, and known in suspect company and is convicted of that, Robert to have the same privilege as if this fault were not pardoned: to which Jonat consents, and binds herself to that by this act, and confessed what was alleged by Robert against her; and on her knees asked forgiveness of him, promising to be a true servant to him and never to fail, and consents to suffer death if she fails him at any time to come. And now the Superintendent commits the woman by supplication to the magistrates of Dysart, where she is resident, for civil punishment, according to the order of that burgh.

August 1564 ... Wyliam Walcar and Jonat Kyninmonth denounced for fornication committed betwixt them, called and appearing they confess the same; and for that fault are ordered to desist from it in future; and for their occasion of having given disgrace are ordered, this next Sunday, in the public congregation of the kirk before noon, during the sermon, to sit upon the penitent stool, and at the end of it, on their knees acknowledge their offences, ask God for mercy and the congregation for forgiveness. And besides this the woman to be committed to the magistrates by supplication, for civil punishment as a common scold, arguer, curser, swearer and filthy person.

[The stool was the "cutty stool" common in every parish as the stool you sat on to be publicly humiliated (naughty stool). Why Jonat was singled out for this treatment is unclear. She may have sworn at the kirk session?]

February 1565 ... About the denunciation given in against Andrew Duncan and Besse Duncan, touching the horrible incest committed betwixt them manifested by procreation of a child between them, the woman being the widow of the late David Fyff nephew of the said Andrew. The parties being summoned by Superintendent's letters to appear and submit to discipline for their offence; the said Andrew appearing personally confesses his fault, humbly submits himself to discipline; and the woman excused by her brother through impediment of a vehement storm of snow at this instant, he in her name confesses her offence, offers himself as surety that she submit to and fulfil the discipline to be enjoined to her. The Superintendent, with advice of the ministry, orders the said Andrew and Bessie three separate Sundays to present themselves in the public assemblies of the kirk of Dron and acknowledge their offences, commit themselves to abstain from all occasion of giving disgrace in future, humble themselves on their knees, ask God for mercy and the congregation for forgiveness; and, in the same manner, three Sundays, make the same satisfaction in the kirk of St Johnstoun [Perth] and pay to the poor box in each kirk 10 shillings.

[Uncle and niece commit incest and have a child together? The six Sundays' penance and 20 shillings perhaps seem a small punishment.]

May 1565 ... Today David Scott and Eufam Wyliamson, being denounced to the Superintendent during his visit for not adhering nor proceeding to the solemnization of their marriage, being under promise of marriage and carnal copulation following upon it, lawfully summoned by the Superintendent's letters to this session, to adhere and proceed to their solemnization of marriage and mutual cohabitation, or else to show some reasonable cause why they should not do so; and appearing, the said Eufame, in presence of David, alleges she should not adhere to him because, after the said promise of marriage and carnal copulation between David and her, and now since reformation of religion, David has given his body to Beatrix Henderson and Besse Dickson, manifested by the procreation of two children betwixt him and the said Beatrix and Besse respectively; and so by adultery committed by David he has cut himself off from her; and therefore she asks to be absolved from adherence, and free to marry in the Lord. David confesses the allegation of giving his body and procreation of children as is alleged, and for his defence alleges the occasion of it was given by Eufam, who absented herself from his company, no occasion made by him to her. The Superintendent, advised by the defence and answer and confession, absolves Eufam from adherence and proceeding to solemnization of mariage with the said David, and commits the said David to be punished by the magistrates according to the law.

August 1565 ... Andrew Weland, in Kilrenny, and Anne Anderson, living in St Andrews, denounced, called and accused as whore-mongers [huyrmongaris]. They confess their offences, showing signs of repentance, are contracted by mutual promise of marriage, and obliged to proceed to solemnization betwixt this and next St Luke's Day [18 October]. They are ordered to make public satisfaction in the assembly of congregation of St Andrews, next Sunday before noon, and their bairn to be received to baptism after noon.

October 1568 ... About the petition given in by Agnes Thomsoun, desiring to have licence to marry anew, notwithstanding that she was divorced of before from Archibald Philp her husband for adultery committed by her, and suffered ecclesiastical discipline and was severely punished for it; the session refused to give licence to her, and referred the judgement of it to the next Assembly of the General Kirk to be held.

[The new Protestant reformers held that adulterers should suffer death and if foolishly spared by the civil authorities should suffer excommunication. They made heavy weather of the question whether adulterers could marry again after reconciliation with the Kirk.]

March 1573 ... John Douglas, Archbishop of St Andrews, was charged in the General Assembly with various faults: "that he was not only Bishop, but Rector of the University, and Provost of the New College; that he preached not in St Andrews, where he made his residence."

In his defence he urged that since the previous Assembly he had been unwell, but promised to preach in the city of St Andrews again, according to his ability ... some weeks later poor Lord Archbishop Douglas finally went into the pulpit in St Andrews to preach ... and fell down dead! One commentator remarked, "Some perhaps may think that a glorious end".

January 1576 ... Robert Grub, younger, witness, examined on the denunciation of Marjory Smyth, spouse of John Pa, accused of witchcraft, sworn, testifies that he heard his own wife, Isobel Johnstoun, and Nannis Michell, report that Isobel Johnstoun, being in labour with her child, Pa's wife came to her and Nannis Michell being there laid her hand on Nannis and she became sick immediately; and the witness's wife being laid up in her bed, she took Nannis by the hand, and she became well again, and ate and drank with the rest of the women there; and testifies that 8 or 9 days later his spouse, being very sick, sent for Pa's wife, and she refused to come until the witness went himself and compelled her to come, and at her coming she took the witness's wife by the arm, and grabbed her, and put her fingers betwixt the parting of her hair, and immediately she called for food: and in addition, testifies that his wife was so sick that none had confidence in her life being oppressed with sweat and vomiting, till Pa's wife came and handled her, and this was four years ago come Whit Sunday. [!]

Christian Methwen, spouse to Walter Padye, cooper, witness, testifies on oath that she was present in Grub's house, when his wife was in the pains of labour and Nannis Michell came in, and after she had asked of Grub's wife her aunt how she did, Pa's wife said she would be well at once, and immediately after Nannis Michell became very sick, and Grub's wife was happier at once and easier of her sickness; and Grub's wife being laid up in her bed Nannis became better: and confesses that they were all scared, and a mist came over the witness's eyes, that she could not see what Pa's wife did to Grub's wife: and further testifies that 9 days later Grub's wife was happier and being very sick, the witness and Robert Grub went for Pa's wife, and made her come and visit Grub's wife, and after she took Grub's wife by the hand she became better and ate and drank.

Andro Sellar and Thomas Christie testify that they desired Johne Pay not to depart from the town if he and his wife's case was good. He answered that he feared, and therefore he and his wife went their ways.

[No further minutes cover this case: it seems Marjory and her husband Pa's case was dropped ... other accusations of witchcraft here were not so lucky!]

August 1576 ... Beaty Strang being called to testify on oath whether the bairn alleged to be begotten between her and William Lermonth was the said William's or not, because the said William referred unconditionally to the said Beaty's oath if the bairn was his.

[Beaty answered and declared the bairn was not his and affirmed it actually belonged to a Frenchman! A servant of the Laird of Ramorny called Rinnie! – René?]

Dec 1576 ... Margaret Marr, spouse to George Richardson, ordered in future to desist from keeping a tavern upon the Sabbath day, under penalty of 40 shillings and make public repentance upon the penitent stool.

June 1577 ... John Millar in Baldinny Mill and Elspet Cwik [Cuik] his spouse accused of putting down a female bairn begotten between them in bond of matrimony by burning the said bairn to death! The said John and Elspeth confess that the bairn was delivered by them to their servant, Elspeth Hay, at about eight at night; she passed out of the inner room of the house with the bairn; half an hour later her goodman and she heard the bairn greet [the baby cry] and said John passed out of the inner room from his own bed, and found the bairn lying by the fire, and Elspeth Hay sleeping, with no clothes except a shirt, which was all burnt except the sleeves, when the bairn was brought by the said John Miller to the said Elspeth Cwik. And John Millar confesses the bairn was burnt, especially upon the back and right shoulder, and died on the 9th day after contracting the burning. Additionally, the said John Millar admits to have had carnal dealings with Elspeth Hay at the previous Lammas [1 August]; and as for the bairn that Elspeth Hay is presently with, the said John Millar refers to the said Elspeth Hay's oath if the bairn be his or not.

[On a crime such as this the bottle dungeon would be used; there is no reaction from the ministers in the files to this crime, which carried the death penalty. I imagine it was transferred to the Edinburgh high courts to finalise.]

1576 ... The General Assembly declared that burials should not be inside the churches, as that was unseemly and not sanitary, desiring a convenient place lying in free air in an area appointed, and the dead to be buried six feet deep!

Sep 1580 ... Mr Robert Hamilton minister and George Black exhorter stated and declared to the session that James Millar, servant to David Orme, confessed and admitted himself to have begotten a bairn with Catherine Bell, desiring them for God's cause to receive his bairn to baptism, and similarly granted the same by a bill produced today before the said session desiring his bairn to be baptised. The session in respect it is understood by them that this is the third time he has committed fornication, they remit him to the secular judge, and to be punished by them according to Act of Parliament.

[It doesn't look good for James Millar, his case moved to Edinburgh, but after being caught fornicating three times, he may have faced the full force of the law ... death by hanging.]

As this diary continues into the latter half of the 1500s we have now new ministers Black and Wallace in the court, who take a stronger stance on the crime of fornication, as we shall see.

August 1583 ... The session, at the reasonable request and desire of the Bishop of St Andrews, desiring their counsel and advice what good arrangement they thought should be made for the examination of Alison Pierson, alleged to be a witch, presently imprisoned, has requested Mr James Wilky, Rector, and George Black, to pass tomorrow to the Presbytery, and desire their good counsel and advice in this, that God may be glorified and vice punished according to the Word of God.

[With the two strict ministers, Alison Pierson never stood a chance!]

March 1583 ... Christine Muir appeared, who admits that she, on 17 March, in the night, passed outside the Southgate Port of this city, and there committed the filthy crime of adultery with James Neilson living in Tess's Mill; and that she also previously committed the filthy vice of adultery with Andrew, Earl of Rothes, and that she bore a female bairn to the said Lord last All Hallows [Alhallowmes] in adultery. The session requests the rector to signify the same to the Presbytery, that arrangements may be made by them, because the transgressors dwell outside their jurisdiction.

[Dear me! Christine Muir has thrown herself around a bit! She seems in serious trouble but no more is found on the case. Andrew Leslie, 5th Earl of Rothes, succeeded his father in 1558, his half-brothers having been disinherited because of their role in the murder of Cardinal Beaton.]

May 1585 ... Elspeth Fogow, accused before the session for smothering her bairn, denies that she smothered the bairn; but says that, 15 weeks ago, her bairn being a male child lying in the bed with her in the night, her bairn died suddenly; but says that her bairn was ten weeks sick before, which she offers to prove. The session orders her to produce proof of it within eight days, she being warned in the proceedings to do this.

A year is missing in the register, no doubt caused by the plague arriving in the city ... one message in the register states ...

"All good order ceased in this city" (see next chapter on the Plague).

*

June 1586 ... Walter Finlayson tailor, grants he has gotten a bairn in fornication with Catherine Kelly, offers to make satisfaction for it, and after that wishes the bairn to be baptised. They are both ordered to be imprisoned, and subsequently to make humiliation.

The session decides to warn James Millar and Bessie Bruce his spouse to appear in eight days to answer to such things as shall be asked them touching their marriage, which is alleged to be incestuous.

[Two weeks later] ... James Steill officer verified that he had warned James Miller and Bessie Bruce to this day personally, to answer to the denunciation given against them, and because they did not appear, they are to be warned to appear, under pain of disobedience, in eight days.

July 1586 ... James Miller appeared, as he was warned to answer to the denunciation given against him in June, who being desired to separate from the company of Elizabeth Bruce his pretended spouse, his first wife's niece with whom he is incestuously married against God's law and order of the Kirk, answers he is not married unlawfully, but with order, and therefore refuses to separate himself. The session ordered him and his pretended spouse to appear before the next synodical assembly in St Andrews to answer to the denunciation.

Dec 1586 ... James Miller, incestuous with Jonet Bruce, produced a supplication from the commissary direct to this session, dated at Edinburgh November last; ... notwithstanding to proceed against the said James and Jonet, in charging them to separate themselves, according to the ordinance of the Assembly; and ordered Jonet Bruce to be warned to appear before them and receive command to separate herself from James; likewise James has also received the same command.

Feb 1587 ... Today Patrick Adamson, Bishop of St Andrews, appeared, alleging himself to have verbal direction of the King's Majesty, to desire the minister and reader to pray for his Highness' mother, for her conversion and amendment of life, and if it be God's pleasure to preserve her from present danger where she is now, that she may hereafter be a profitable member in Christ's kirk. The session presently assembled, being sufficiently resolved herewith, has concluded that the minister at each sermon, and the reader at each time when he says the prayers, pray publicly for the King's Grace's mother as is desired.

[This kirk session met at two in the afternoon, but at eight that morning Mary Queen of Scots had been beheaded in England! ... so the Protestant ministers in St Andrews would have prayed for the Catholic Queen after her death.]

May 1587 ... James Miller appeared before the session, and confessed that he is now moved by God's spirit and surely persuaded that he has done wrong in marrying Elizabeth Bruce, his first wife's niece, and is now surely warned that the same is incest; and therefore is content to separate himself from her company, and to enter on the penitent stool next Sunday with the said Elizabeth, and make humiliation in sackcloth according to the ordinance of the kirk and to continue till the Church is satisfied.

July 1588 ... Today appeared Agnes Melville daughter to the late Andrew Melville elder and former reader at Anstruther Kirk. Born in Anstruther from Margaret Wood her mother, of age 34 or 35 years, being denounced as a suspect of witchcraft, admits that she was first married with a man called Steven Crichton, former mariner of Anstruther; and that she is now married to David Banis, son to David Banis citizen of St Andrews; and that she lived all her days in Anstruther except this last year she lived in Crail; and now she remains in St Andrews, as she has done since 15 days before last Whit Sunday; and now declares she had Thomas, child to her second husband, and that it is 11 years since she was married with David Banis, but that she kept house with him except three or four years; and thereafter she came and lived with John Kynneir in Kingask one summer season; and then half a year with his mother; and thereafter in and out with Mr Thomas Beinston's wife in Pittenweem, six weeks or thereabouts; and thereafter in North Berwick, with the good wife's daughter of Lundy Mill, a quarter of a year or thereabouts; and then with her mother again, half a year; and thereafter she came to Crail, where she lived six weeks with Alexander Wilson's wife altogether; and thereafter came to St Andrews, and remained with Agnes and Elspot Farleis twenty weeks coming and going, before the plague in St Andrews; and then passed to Anstruther, and remained with her father and mother two years; and then to Crail, where she remained till 15 days before last Whitsunday; and then came to St Andrews, where she still remains.

The said Agnes being asked by the minister, in presence of the whole session, convened with Mr Thomas Buchanan and Mr John Caldcleuch, as they who are direct from the Presbytery, if she has skill and knowledge of herbs, answers, Yea, she has skill with parsley, spring onions, comfrey, wormwood, elecampane and of a herb called *concilarum* [probably scurvy grass]; and declares that she has used spring onions, parsley and comfrey to help various people who have had evil stomachs; and especially that she used this cure on Janet Spens, spouse of John Symson in Crail.

Being asked if she knows the powers of stones, denies.

Being asked what power is between south-running water and other water – she knows not, but hears say south-running water should be used.

[This water superstition prevailed in Scotland at the time, running water being known pure, especially south-running water. It was the main reason England had so many drowned witches, a witch being impure should float when dunked in water, therefore to drown would prove you weren't a witch. There was no easy way out once accused as a witch.]

Being asked if she helped Catherine Pryde in Crail of her disease and sickness, she answers that Catherine Pryde had a disease and sickness which was a consumption of the stomach, and that she made a drink of spring onions parsley and comfrey, steeped in ale 24 hours, and gave her to drink, who drank it for eight days; and after that wished her to wash herself with water and specially south-running water; and when she had washed herself with the water, bade her throw the water on the midden, for feet water should not be thrown in anybody's way.

Declares that she learnt the knowledge of herbs and specially the herb called *concilarum*, in North Berwick, from a man called Mr John ——, who was an old man gathering herbs behind a dyke in North Berwick; and that he had a wife as he said to her, and dwellt in Edinburgh. And she, being gathering corn at the time, saw him gathering herbs, and she said to him, What kind of herb is this? He answered, They call it *concilarum*. I pray you sir, tell me what is this herb good for? He answered, give me a pint of ale, and I shall tell you. And she said, I only have a bawbee, which she gave him. And says she never saw him before or since, and that he then asked her what they called her and where she dwellt; and also declares that Mr John showed her that south-running water is best, and better than other water; and that the same is good to wash folks from the knees and elbows down, and good to help their hurt stomach; and says that she vomited when she left North Berwick; and that Mr John taught her to take spring onions, parsley and two blades of comfrey, and *concilarum*, to make a drink of, and taught her to make drinks with it.

And further declares that John Melville's wife in Crail taught her to take white bread with water and sugar, to help to staunch the vomit, and says she learnt nothing else from anybody.

[The mention of Agness not splashing herself with water shows the suspicions of the court, witches being scared of water. She was let off from the accusations at this date, being Andrew Melville's daughter, who was brother to James Melville, Beaton's murderer. She was one of the two women brought forward to help the afflicted Archbishop Patrick Hamilton. Being accused of being a witch was a stigma that could come back and haunt at a later date, but her status as one of the Melville family probably saved her ... for now!]

Oct 1588 ... Beatrix Delarasche admits she is with bairn to James Brand son of John Brand minister of the Canongate; the bairn was gotten last Easter in John Scheve's house in this city; and that she never knew him carnally except once in the chamber. Missive is ordered to be sent to John Brand for trial.

[The minister (1564–1600) John Brand had been a monk at Holyrood Abbey. He had another son John who in

1615 while a student at the College of Philosophy in Edinburgh had "slaughtered" William King, natural son of James King, advocate – he stabbed him to death and was sentenced to be beheaded.]

Sep 1589 ... The session orders Issobel Strang to be warned to come to the stool of repentance next Sunday, for fornication with William Arthur, under penalty of public admonition; and also to warn the said William and Isobel to answer in eight days' time to answer to a new denunciation, to wit, for new carnal copulation.

Sep 1589 ... Issobel Strang being warned to this day, as she was four separate times previously, to have appeared to give her reasons why she does not satisfy the kirk for fornication with William Arthur of Carnis, as was verified by Andrew Sellar, officer, she did not appear. Therefore the session ordered her to be publicly summoned for eight days hence, under penalty of the kirk's censure, for the first public admonition.

Oct 1590 ... Thomas Wood reader produced a summons duly executed and endorsed by him last Sunday, with Issobel Strang summoned to this day, to give her reasons why she does not obey the voice of the kirk, and does not satisfy for fornication with William Arthur of Carnis. Issobel being often called, not appearing, reluctant to my bidding, the session ordered summons to be sent to summon her to make public humiliation next Sunday, for the second public admonition, under penalty of the kirk's censure.

May 1590 ... Issobel Strang admits she has recently borne a bairn in fornication, within this quarter of a year, to William Arthur of Carnis; and this is the second bairn she has borne to him. She is ordered to be imprisoned for 15 days, and to satisfy according to the order; and William is to be warned for the third time to answer the denunciation.

Oct 1590 ... At the earnest supplication of Issobel Strang, desiring herself to be received to repentance for the bairn gotten on her in fornication by the late William Arthur of Carnis, and afterwards her bairn to be baptised, the session ordered her to pay 20 shillings in part payment of the Act for her imprisonment, and to sit two separate Sundays on the stool of repentance, and after that her bairn to be baptised.

May 1591 ... Walter Geddy, being called before the session to make public humiliation in sackcloth for the unhappy slaughter of the late James Cockburn, appeared, and offered himself willing to obey anything the kirk would enjoin to him for the same; but alleges various reasons to continue public humiliation for a specified time, which being heard and found reasonable, the session continued his public humiliation till next Lammas.

[It seems to be an accident that resulted in James Cockburn's death.]

May 1591 ... Andrew Todd in Strathkinness, servant to John Richard there, for breaking and violating the last Sabbath day in digging and sowing flax, against the law of God, is ordered to sit on a stool low in the kirk, beneath the place of repentance, upon Sunday before noon, and stand up after the sermon, and make public humiliation, and ask God and the congregation for forgiveness.

May 1591 ... Alexander Dick and Elspeth Lessellis adulterers are ordered to appear next Sunday, at the second bell to sermon before noon, and stand there clad in sackcloth till the last bell stops ringing, and to ascend the highest step on the penitent stool, and sit till the sermon, prayer and blessing have been given, and so forth to continue each Sunday till the kirk be satisfied.

[Greater degrees of badness meant the higher up the penitent stool you had to go; most had three steps.]

Oct 1591 ... Today the sentence of excommunication against Janet Paty and Catherine Patrick to be pronounced.

[This case has dragged on for three months. Janet has produced a baby and even with the Sheriff appearing to her with summons letters in person she hasn't turned up in court. Excommunication was your baptism rights removed from you, and banished from the city.]

Oct 1591 ... John Smyth and Margaret Fleming admit they have gotten a bairn together in fornication, in David Smyth's house in this city; and that the same bairn was born in Lokkeis house in this city and the bairn was born dead and buried under silence of night by Andrew Sellar and Alan, bellman. The session ordered them to satisfy for their offence according to the order; and Andrew Sellar and Alan to be warned for burying of the bairn, being gotten in fornication and without satisfaction made to the kirk for that, and under silence of night, the magistrates not being alerted.

[Andrew Sellar is the court Sherriff.]

[Nov 1591 – Feb 1593 ... Nothing but endless fornicator crimes. I will omit these years to avoid repetition; it seems a plague of fornicating was jamming up the church courts.]

Feb 1593 ... Today George Scott, gardener, and Andrew Scott, quarryman, admonished for extraordinary drinking and misspending of their property, and commanded to spend their property at home with their wives and bairns reasonably.

Feb 1593 ... Today Christine Johnstone appeared, who admits she has borne a bairn in fornication to David Anderson, which was gotten in the over Abbey Mill. The said David present admits the same, and that this is the third bairn that he's gotten in fornication. He is ordered to pay 40 shillings for his imprisonment, and to satisfy the kirk, and all satisfaction according to the Act of Parliament, that a man three times relapsed in fornication ought to do.

[He would be banished the city.]

[Minister David Black has started on the sessions, he and another minister Wallace take a stronger stance on lawbreakers in future.]

Mar 1594 ... David Thompson in Balgoif appeared, who admits he has gotten a bairn in fornication with Jonet Schiphirt. He is ordered to be imprisoned and yoked, or else to pay 40 pounds to the poor. David has made humiliation, as also Jonet Schippart, but he has paid only 8 pounds!

[Probably everything he had.]

April 1594 ... It was denounced to the session that David Leys son of John Leys, blacksmith, had put hand on and struck his father, because of which the session requested the magistrates to call him before them, and to put him to an appropriate hearing according to the laws; which request the magistrates most willingly obeyed, and David Leys was convicted at an appropriate hearing, and ordered to appear in sackcloth, bareheaded and barefoot, upon the highest step of the penitent stool with a hammer in one hand and a stone in the other hand, as two instruments with which he menaced his father, with a paper written in great letters about his head saying: "Behold the unnatural son punished for putting hand in his father and dishonouring of God in him". After that to appear in the middle of the kirk on Sunday and ask forgiveness from God, his father and the whole people; and after that on Monday to stand from ten until twelve noon, clad and adorned as said, in the jougs at the mercat cross; and after that to be carted through the whole town, and the people to be advised and informed of his fault by open proclamation, and after that brought again to the cross and his indictment read and published, with these words: "If he ever offend against his father or mother, in word or deed, that member of his body with which he offends shall be cut off from him, be it tongue, hand or foot, without mercy, in example to others to abstain from the like."

May 1594 ... Alexander Wood appeared and submits himself to discipline, for begetting of a bairn in fornication with Elspet Russel. He is ordered to pay £40 within 48 hours, for the satisfaction of the Act of Parliament, and to make public humiliation according to the order; and James Wood his father to be warned to pay 40 shillings for not revealing the fault of the said Alexander his son. – Alexander has made humiliation and paid £24.

Nov 1594 ... Clearly verified and proven before the session that John Grey, smith, has spoken diverse and sundry blasphemous and wicked words against God, Mr David Black and Mr Robert Wallace, ministers. The said John sat down on his knees and in presence of the whole session asked God for mercy and the said ministers for forgiveness; and is ordered with his own consent, if ever he in future is offensive or offends the ministers or any members of the session in word or deed, that he shall make public satisfaction as adulterers are used to in sackcloth, and pay a sum to the poor box at the discretion of the session and magistrates.

[Wallace and Black's hard stance is being criticized in public, one such speaker was John Grey above]

1594 ... The session has ordered and decreed Arthur Miln barrel-maker deacon and Andrew Cuik butcher, for their misbehaviour, and unreverend speeches and language in session, to sit upon a stool before the pulpit the whole time of sermon next Sunday; and after that they to ask God for mercy, the whole session and congregation for forgiveness: and if either of them fails in the like fault after this, he that fails to sit half a year upon the penitent stool in sackcloth.

Apr 1595 ... Today John Smyth merchant called before the session for striking of Jonet Guidlaid his spouse, and misbehaving to her, to the dishonour of God and disgrace of the congregation, he appeared and confesses the same. The session ordered him to pay £3 to the poor box, and he is obliged by his own consent, if he ever do the like offence to his wife in future, to pay to the poor box £10 as often as he transgresses. – John paid 20 shillings at once in part payment of the £3.

March 1595 ... Today John Ross, master of the song school, most humbly, with all reverence on his knees before the session, asked God for mercy and the Kirk forgiveness for his negligence, for his using and playing a part of the comedy and play in St Leonards College ... by advice of the kirk; as also Mr John Heklein, regent to the bachelors, and Mr John Dowglas, pedagogue to my Lord Buchan, confess, in presence of the session, that it was against their will that the same play was played; and promise hereafter to stop and withstand all such things in their power, and never to do the like in future. And therefore the session orders John Ross's humiliation, and their declaration and promise, to be published to the people next Sunday.

[An over-exuberant actor practising his art!]

May 1595 ... Alison Downy, Bessy Miller, Beigis Watson and Catherine Geddy, midwives, being called and appearing before the session, are commanded, when they or any of them are charged to be midwives to any woman, that they ask the woman with bairn diligently who is the bairn's father; and if the bairn is not gotten in lawful marriage, that they at once inform the ministers, elders and deacons of the kirk, under penalty of 40 shillings, with their own consent, to the poor box.

May 1595 ... Today Andrew Sellar, officer to the kirk session, being called, accused and convicted for his ungodly and unreverend behaviour and speeches in session, is decreed to sit next Sunday, time of sermon, before noon, clad in sackcloth, upon a stool before the pulpit, and afterwards ask God, the whole session and congregation for forgiveness.

[Andrew has been bullying others using his position as court sheriff: it has not gone down well among the ministers. For others who Andrew has arrested and brought to the session courts this must have been very satisfying.]

July 1595 ... Elane Hamilton, daughter of the late Robert Hamilton [probably a former minister of St Andrews] after a long process and frequent denial at last admits she has had a female bairn born in fornication with the late Robert Hamilton, sometime minister of Kennoway, and that the bairn was born dead. The session and magistrates ordered her to pay £6 in part payment of the Act for her imprisonment, and to make public humiliation according to the order.

[Dear oh dear ... this huge payment shows she was in jail a considerable time, but the shame of her confession explains why she refused to tell for so long!]

Sep 1595 ... Issobel Annell is instructed to make public humiliation for fetching Agness Melville, a condemned witch, to consult with her to cure the late Patrick Wyle her spouse; also Issobel Symsoun for seeking the said late Agnes Melville and for consulting with her to cure the late John Black her spouse. And James Chaiplane is instructed to make public humiliation for fetching the late Jonet Lochequoir, a condemned witch, to cure John Richart's wife in Strathkinness. And John Weddell younger is instructed to make public humiliation for fetching the late Elspot Gilcrist, a condemned witch, to cure the late Jonet Horsburth in Balmungie.

[Agness was one of the two women brought by James Melville her uncle to help heal Archbishop Hamilton in 1588. Alison Pierson was the one credited with finally curing the Archbishop, and Alison would have her kindness and skills thrown back at her with accusations of witchcraft, and would be tortured and would burn for it! Agness, with the position of her uncle and her minister father Andrew Melville, was protected from the wrath of the church, although she was accused also. James died; then by 1595 her father is mentioned as being the "late Speaker in Anstruther Kirk". Without the protection of her father and uncle she was accused again and this time was burned in 1595 in St Andrews. The aftermath of her trial was finding those who also took advice and paid for her services, as the above people are charged, the 1563 Witchcraft Act states "no person seek ony help response or consultation at anysuch users of witchcraft sorcery or necromancy under pain of deid". The people who paid for Agness's skills are lucky the St Andrews Kirk, under the order of strict minister rule from Wallace and Black, only got public humiliation! ... It could have easily led to a death sentence.]

April 1596 ... William Vtein to make public humiliation Sunday next for breaking of the Sabbath by extraordinary drinking and for rash wicked speaking!

May 1596 ... Today being appointed to try the life and conversation of the whole members of the session as well ministers as elders and deacons – Mr David Black minister being sent out, there is nothing objected against him, but all the brethren praise God of him, and that he may continue in his way, and Robert Wallace being sent out, the brethren thank God for him, but it is desired of him that he may be more diligent and careful over the manners of the people, and in visiting of the sick.

[Ministers Black and Wallace's tough stance has finally gone too far, other ministers who do not share the pairs strong condemnation of petty crimes are themselves being slandered by the pair from Sunday sessions.]

October 1596 ... The Presbytery ordains the trial of all their members, beginning at St Andrews. Mr David Black was removed, and the judgement of the brethren craved concerning him in doctrine, life and conversation. Three of the brethren had faults to lay against him; but, on his answers being heard and considered by the said persons, they were fully satisfied and contented with them.

Some of the Provincial Assembly held at Dysart had been offended with the said Mr David, by reason of divers reports which had come to their ears, namely, that Mr David in his sermons inveighed against ministers, in his sermons calling some of them – pint-ale ministers, belly-fellows, sycophants, gentlemen's ministers, leaders of the people to Hell; and that a great part of them were worthy to be hanged!

David did answer to the accusations: "whatever he had spoken he had spoken it in no ways to disgrace any man's person and office".

[David Black and Wallace were removed by King James VI himself, charged with "speaking his mind too freely before the prime courts".]

August 1596 ... Today William Geddy appeared and, being accused of drinking extraordinarily and wicked talk, confessed the same and craved God, and the kirk in the name of the congregation, forgiveness; and is of his own voluntary consent and free will bound, obliged and recorded, not only to abstain from the like in future, but, if he is found guilty in the like, to make public humiliation and pay £10 to the poor.

October 1596 ... Today Walter Geddy, after he had made public humiliation according to the ordinance of the synodal assembly for the cruel slaughter of the late James Cockburn, was received to repentance publicly, clad in sackcloth upon the penitent stool.

[It looks like a fight has taken place with James Cockburn being killed, the church's stance here is very slight with repentance only being demanded.]

Feb 1598 ... Thomas Studwart called and accused of resetting [harbouring] in his house Agnes Jack a filthy fornicatrix, she being already banished from the city, confessed the same; and therefore he is ordered, by advice of the magistrates, to put her from his house, under penalty of banishment himself.

April 1598 ... Gelis Smyth appeared, being accused to declare who was father of the baby in her belly, answered Robert Shivez, son of her master James Shivez, was the father of it; and that he had to do with her carnally 8 days immediately before he sailed for France, and so by her own reckoning it is 29 weeks since the bairn was gotten.

July 1598 ... It was charged that Gelis Smyth, in time of her labouring with child, confessed the same to have been gotten by James Shivez, notwithstanding she alleged earlier the same to have been gotten by Robert Shives his son; and for the better trial thereof, certain of the brethren being directed to pass to her and try the verity thereof, she being bedfast in Mutto's Wynd; who, being examined, confessed that the same bairn then borne by her was gotten by the said James Shives and by no other person, and that he had carnal copulation with her three separate times, 14 days or so before Michaelmas last.

July 1598 ... Thomas Moreis being called, appeared and being accused, confessed the violating of the Sabbath day. He is admonished that if he is tried in future to be a breaker of the Sabbath day, a drunkard, a fighter or a night walker, disobedient to magistrates, or doing such things as do not become a Christian, that he shall be publicly declared an unworthy member of this congregation and punished appropriately for it.

Chapter 7

The Plague Years

When Regulus' boat crashed into the rocks in St Andrews Bay, it changed the barren area called the "Land of Boars" as well as the face of Scotland forever, and another boat landing in this area nearly 1,300 years later, in 1585, would also change the face of Scotland and St Andrews.

On board, an illness had taken the crew. Once the boat was in St Andrews harbour and unloaded, the disease spread from household to household, some people dying within hours of this rapid, violent, strange pestilence. Out of a population of six thousand souls living within the safety of its walls, four thousand would be taken by this unearthly shadow of death in St Andrews alone!

Edinburgh had been the first Scottish place to experience this, in the year 1568, from a merchant boat docking in the harbour from an English port, and it would linger in the country for the next 30 years.

The typical symptoms of plague described in 1569 were swooning, cold sweats, vomiting, corrupt and tough excrement, urine black in colour, cramp, convulsion of limbs, imperfection of speech, stinking breath, swellings of the body, red spots quickly discovered and covering themselves – then death!

The Scottish government brought out some guidelines to combat the plague

1 ... No stranger to enter a town without a certificate of health.

2 ... No furniture to be removed from an infected house.

3 ... No public gatherings.

4 ... All houses to be kept clean of filth.

5 ... All fires in moveable pans, the air to be burnt by convenient fumes.

6 ... No unwholesome meats, stinking fish, flesh or musty corn to be exposed in the shops.

7 ... No swine, dogs, cats or pigeons to pass up or down streets of infected places.

8 ... No more ale houses be licensed than absolutely necessary, especially during this time of present contagion.

9 ... That each city and town forthwith provide a convenient place remote from the same where if infection breaks out people can be searched for signs of the pestilence, viz swellings or risings under ears or armpits or upon the groin, carbuncles or spots either on the breast or back, commonly called tokens.

10 ... That if a house be infected, the sick person to be removed forthwith to the said pest house. The

infected house to be shut up for 40 days and have a red cross painted over the door and "Lord have mercy upon us" painted.

11 ... After 40 days the infected house is to have a white cross painted on the door and remain for twenty days more. The house to be well fumed, and bleached all over within with lime, no clothes or household stuff to be touched for three whole months at least.

12 ... None dying of the plague to be buried in churches or churchyards, a place dug ten foot deep to be filled with lime and graves to be not opened for at least a year least they infect others.

13 ... To take special care of monthly fasts, and public prayers on Wednesdays and Fridays; with this God may be inclined to remove his severe hand both from among you and us.

Dr Chambers, who wrote the *Domestic Annals of Scotland*, gives a complete description of the health practices in Edinburgh during this period.

According to custom in Edinburgh, the families which proved to be infected were compelled to remove with all their goods and furniture out to the burgh moor where they lodged in wretched huts hastily erected for their accommodation. They were allowed to be visited by friends, in company with an officer, after eleven in the morning. Anyone going earlier was liable to be punished by death! Infected clothes were purified by boiling in a large cauldron erected in the open air. Two carers were chosen to aid the sufferers called Bailies of the Muir, each dressed in a gown of grey with a white St Andrews cross on the front and back.

The 1569 epidemic in Edinburgh would carry away 2,500 with the disease in a year. Although that was a huge number of people, in the city of London's packed streets the plague was killing a hundred a night. The mortality rate was terrible in built-up areas. Where people congregated together the disease exploded in the summer months, taking almost forty percent of the population.

The disease came to individual villages, but measures were usually taken to contain the disease to the one house, so everyone inside but only those inside could get infected. Here is an example of this kind of attempt at quarantine from the Pittenweem council records of 1645 ...

> 27th June ... the bailies and counsel ordain John Swyne to remain with his hail famile within his house, for trial that he be free of the pestilence during the bailies' pleasure, and that he suffer none to come in his house unless he detain them as his own.

An armed guard would be set by the house with shoot-to-kill orders if anyone set foot outside. These measures helped contain the disease, but were impossible to use in a city.

The clergy were traditionally present at the passing and death of one of St Andrews' citizens, giving the last rites. This close contact with the infected took a terrible toll on the priests and clergy. Walter Bower the historian recorded that 24 men, about a third of the canons of St Andrews, died in the outbreak, of who all but three were priests. This is a remarkably high proportion and would have been similar in other parishes. In England forty-five percent of the clergy died. It was a significant problem, as we could see in the previous chapter where we lost a year in the parish session records. A statement in the register suggests utter calamity!

1586 *die penultimo menses Junii*

An entry under this date where a year has disappeared from the ledger says ...

"all guid order has cessit in this city"

The plague had arrived in St Andrews in 1585 and within a year had fully taken over, with not enough living people around to bury the dead! General order had collapsed by the time a year had passed, as the plague rampaged through the city. St Andrews was chaos. All order was lost.

Walter Bower records that "people who died from the disease in St Andrews were men of ample education, circumspect in spiritual and in temporal matters upright and honourable in their way of life". Bower talks of the "churchmen in St Andrews now carrying weapons, engaging in dancing and celebrating extra masses purely for nothing but financial gain".

With the sick reaching out for the benefits of the church with prayers, and full sacraments proving useless as prevention, scared and shocked by the numbers of dead, the priests meanwhile took full advantage of the enclosed abbeys to feel safe and free from the pestilence raging outside. When all around them on the streets death was at hand, it is no surprise that many of the St Andrews clergy lost faith and indulged themselves, knowing that their last days on earth might not be far away, because of this invisible death that seemed to strike their comrades at will!

One hundred years later the plague would appear again in Edinburgh. So scared were they from its previous appearance, that the Scottish Parliament moved to St Andrews, setting up in the College of St John for a year in 1645. It's still called Parliament Hall today.

It would take a few hundred years before scientists made the connection with fleas infected by blood carrying the disease, jumping from the warmth of one dying body to another close by.

As with other cities inflicted with the pestilence where the numerous dead could no longer be buried individually, deep plague pits were dug so that the bodies could be dumped in mass graves. Once the plague had finally dissipated and died down in Scotland ... one third of the population was dead.

The ruins of St Andrews Cathedral are surrounded by a thick wall that runs round its circumference and still stands proud today. But at one junction of the wall there is a square tower, that differs in form from all the others. It has an outside stair, peculiarly conceived, that leads to a chamber shaped, like that beneath it, in the figure of the letter L. The building is three storeys high, and in 1826 curiosity got the better of some students who broke open the wall of the tower and entered the chamber inside.

A professor of the United Colleges found the figure of a dead woman in a coffin, looking as though she had died within the hour, so mummified had her body become in the airless conditions of the tomb. Twelve further corpses were found round the walls, also in remarkable condition. The room was sealed up, and not entered again until 1868, when the tomb was reopened by Mr Hall, an inspector of the college. "We found a square chamber with a recess westward in the body of the wall in which was a number of coffins containing bodies, the coffins being piled one over the other. The bodies – about ten in number – which we examined were in a wonderful state of preservation. They had become dried and sufficiently stiff to be lifted up and set on end. Some of them appeared to be wrapped in linen, and had undergone a sort of embalming. One, a female, had on her a set of white gloves very entire. Some of the coffins were of sturdy oak and some wax cloth remains were in them. Nothing was found to indicate who they were or when they had been laid there."

With news of the discovery spreading around the ale houses in St Andrews, it was merely a matter of time before the thoughts of the missing relics – St Andrew's bones – and hidden monks' treasures from the time of John Knox's sermons came to the minds of common thieves and cutpurses. Before long the coffins were found smashed and damaged – the mummified lady had been stolen. All that was rescued from the chaos of vandalism was one foot from the resting lady. The foot was on display at the College Museum for a while. This author is unclear as to its location today.

Many skulls and bones were found in the lower reaches of the tower by a Professor Heddle and Doctor Traill, and when assessing the skulls it was found that many had their jaws tied up in strings to prevent the mouths opening. Although first thoughts were tooth decay, all had fine examples of teeth in splendid condition. David Henry, who wrote a book called *Mediaeval St Andrews*, did some research and found that the room had originally been built joined to the monastery, which it overlooked. Although any wording on the tomb is now indecipherable, it belonged to a woman called Katherine Clephane, wife of

John Martine of Denbrae. They were known to have died from the plague in 1605.

This tomb was built for those two and other victims, and was sealed up because of the belief that to reopen it would be to let the disease go forth and its misery continue. That was the reason it was left unopened till 1826.

With the discovery of the "white lady", gossipmongers spread the news from tavern to tavern around St Andrews. It wasn't long before white ghostly figures were said to be seen walking around the cathedral graveyard, starting a trend of reports of phantom women pacing to and fro terrifying the locals, and walking the dark streets at night. Even today the white lady is still said to be seen now and again. Rudely disturbed from her rest all those years ago ... many books mention her, and students still feel uneasy walking near here at night.

Chapter 8

The Brutal Murder of Archbishop Sharp

In the Holy Trinity Kirk in St Andrews may be seen a vast tomb, set in black and white marble, that extends from the floor to the roof. It was designed by a Dutch mason and built at the expense of the son of the dead man residing in it. This is the tomb of Archbishop Sharp!

Archbishop Sharp's tomb in 1725 was broken into and damaged in an act of wanton vandalism by several unknown men. They had a determination about them to fish out the archbishop's bones and run off into the night with them. All this violence to a man who had by then been dead for nearly fifty years! In May 1679 the archbishop had been attacked and killed on a flat plain just outside St Andrews – a flat, grassy area called Magnus Moor. But a bitter hatred for this man obviously lingered for a few years yet.

His murder was committed by a party of nine men who had set out that day to kill another – the Sheriff of Fife, William Carmichael. They had planned the ambush at a secluded spot away from prying eyes and had hidden in amongst the trees at Magnus Moor, but before Carmichael had arrived news came of a bigger fish! A young boy came on foot with news that the archbishop himself, James Sharp, the man who had given the sheriff his position, was only a few miles away and fast heading in the direction of the moor!

His horsedrawn carriage, when near enough, was then attacked, the Archbishop dragged out from his comfort screaming, with his daughter trying to protect him. He was dispatched like a farm animal with sixteen wounds to his body, as his daughter held on to him. Such was the prize for the nine assassins.

Before we judge a murder as brutal as this we must see where all this hatred came from, and for that we go back a few years from 1679 to Charles I's reign when, in 1638, the National Covenant was signed.

The National Covenant was a promise or contract to undertake to defend the church, the Presbyterian establishment and the king. It was deliberately set out to crush the king's claim of "divine right". It contained three parts ...

1. A commitment to renounce Catholic beliefs and practices and a pledge to uphold Presbyterianism.

2. The second part contained a huge list of statutes and acts by which the Presbyterian Church had been established.

3. Free Parliaments and assemblies (not usurped by the king's meddling and rigged by him as was customary). It pledged its signatories to disregard Charles' recent innovations, and to defend the religion against all persons whatsoever.

It removed the king's claim of divine right and held Protestantism above the king.

*

Charles I took huge offence and war started. He pressed for Episcopalian measures, i.e. a more Catholic, or Anglican Church, way of arranging things: a church run by bishops, in which royal supremacy was assumed in ecclesiastical cases. The king had divine right over the church.

Civil war started and was finally finished when Oliver Cromwell had the king dispatched for treason against his people in 1649. Cromwell ruled instead for the next nine years till his death in 1658. Two years later, in 1660, Charles II was invited to take the throne.

Charles II's restoration was highly popular in Scotland among all ranks and the most extravagant rejoicing prevailed everywhere. Most of the rejoicing was from the Presbyterians who were his most devoted supporters; much pain had been endured during the Cromwell years, with Scotland heavily taxed to cover war expenses. Charles had sworn the National League and Covenant and had engaged to maintain the government and privileges of the Church of Scotland. But unknown to all, Charles's views were the same as the past monarch Charles I, and secretly he hated Protestantism because it limited his monarchical powers in favour of liberty. He concealed his hypocritical views until he was restored to the crown. Then the opportunity arose for him to violate his promise, ungratefully insulting the Protestants who had supported him.

An act of Parliament was passed, "The Act of Supremacy", making the king supreme judge in all matters civil and ecclesiastical. Next he restored the church's rule by bishops. There was uproar in Edinburgh when this act was accomplished, nearly 400 ministers refused the oath, as it was "inconsistent with the principals they had solemnly sworn to maintain in which it was founded on the word of

God not the king"! The ministers were speedily ejected from their own parishes and replaced by "Episcopal" ministers who supported the king's views.

But the evicted ministers took their faithful flocks to the fields and preached in barns and in the open air in total defiance of the king. In 1663 a new law came out: "The Act against separation and disobedience to ecclesiastical authority". It made it illegal to preach in contempt of the law. Another law came in 1670 making it a crime of treason ... it now merited a death sentence to preach against the king's stance. Treason.

Instead of changing the minds of the people and extinguishing the Presbyterian cause, it had exactly the opposite effect. Open rebellion followed risings in the Pentland Hills. People rushed to sign their own covenant (or promise) listing their names in thousands around the country opposing Episcopal rule.

In St Andrews a copy of the solemn League and Covenant is still preserved in the University. It bears the signatures of 981 men. They include magistrates, professors, students, citizens and parishioners. Fifteen names are marked by crosses, as the men were illiterate.

Many lists of the signed covenant were handed in as protests, and so the king's supporters now had a list, albeit a huge one, of traitors against the crown, all signed in their own hands, and King Charles had advocates picked by him to hunt down the people who had their signatures on the Covenants.

One of Charles' deputies employed in the Covenant hunt was Archbishop Sharp, who employed the Sheriff Carmichael to do his brutal work hunting down the covenanters, with no mercy.

The archbishop had originally been a minister from a parish in Crail in Fife, and so trusted was he that he was selected to read the terms to Charles II in London about the survival of Protestantism in Scotland. The deal seemed secure, but Charles changed his mind, as did Minister James Sharp when offered consecration as Archbishop of St Andrews from Charles.

Instantly he swapped Presbyterianism for Episcopacy, gaining the riches to be had as head of the clergy in St Andrews.

The archbishop appointed William Carmichael as his Sheriff and now with the backing of the king started to hunt down those who had signed the Covenant, and those avoiding church, going to illegal Protestant preachings instead. Carmichael tortured the wives and children of the signers of the Covenant to find them and bring them to his own justice, stealing any wealth found in the farms and houses along the way, making himself very rich and very hated.

On Magnus Moor near St Andrews, the nine assassins waited in the trees. The original target of Carmichael the sheriff was now left behind and thoughts of murder were aimed at the approaching Archbishop of St Andrews, a much bigger fish! The waiting assassins were...

David Hackstone of Rathillet, John Balfour of Kinloch (brother-in-law to David Hackston), James Russell of Kingskettle, William Dingwall of Cadden, George Flemming of Balboathy, Andrew and Alexander Henderson of Kilbrachmont, George Balfour (called Burley from Gilston), William Daniel.

An assassination attempt had already been carried out ten years prior to this in 1668 when James Mitchell took a pistol to the hated archbishop in his coach in Edinburgh. On 11th July Mitchell saw the archbishop leave his lodgings at Blackfriars Wynd, walked up to the coach, leant in and fired. He missed, but hit the archbishop's friend the Bishop of Orkney in the hand. Mitchell would casually walk away into the shadows of Edinburgh but be caught in 1674 again with a loaded pistol. Because he acted suspiciously he was apprehended. He was brutally tortured by "the boot", a hellish wooden device designed to crush the leg bones of a man. He confessed all, and was imprisoned on the Bass Rock, which was an island prison in the Forth estuary, and executed in January 1678 by hanging.

On Friday 2nd May, Archbishop Sharp set out from Edinburgh with his daughter Isabel in his horse-drawn coach with him. They reached the village of Kennoway by evening, and bedded down for the night at Captain Seton's house (the building was still standing until 1951). On the Saturday morning they continued towards St Andrews, but along the way a boy who knew the covenanters lying waiting for the sheriff brought news of the approaching archbishop's coach.

The assassins cried at the news, "Truly this is of God!" and organised the ambush... The coach came within reach where they sprang out the trees, James Russell firing both his pistols into the carriage crying, "Judas be taken!" Sharp's servant was instantly disarmed and the archbishop was pulled by many hands outside the carriage. His daughter threw herself in front of her father to protect him from the assault, but her heroic efforts were not enough: she was knocked aside with a wound to her hands. "Thou are taken, Judas, thou are taken," Burley shouted as he rode his horse over him, while Russell hacked at his head with a sword. A local weaver Andrew Gullan happened to arrive at the point of the murder. He pleaded for the archbishop's life, but it was too late, as others dirked Sharp on the ground until sixteen wounds had been given and the primate was a bloody soaking mess!

On inspection in St Andrews he was found to have stab wounds on his back, slash wounds to his head, a cut above his left eye, three in his left hand, a gunshot wound above his right breast.

The assassins withdrew to a nearby cottage where they rejoiced at putting what they saw as a warlock to death. With news spreading of the archbishop's murder a huge manhunt for the murderers was now in full swing.

The Covenanters regrouped near Darvel in Ayrshire where Robert Hamilton was appointed to be their leader; they had around 300 poorly equipped men. At Drumclog Moor 150 mounted soldiers under John Graham of Claverhouse were sent to deal with them and arrest the leaders. They met and discharged weapons at point-blank range, one of the government men being killed. The horses were sent to flank the Covenanters, but got stuck in the muddy conditions turning the charge into a farce. The Covenanters charged the stricken enemy, chasing the soldiers from the field, killing around forty. Another twelve were killed in flight and five were captured. The Covenanters lost one man in the battle and another five of wounds later. One of the five was one of Archbishop Sharp's assassins who charged the dragoons ... William Daniel.

With the Covenanters victorious, John Balfour and David Hackston attacked Glasgow from two directions, losing seven men as Glasgow manned its defences. The rebels fell back to a place called Bothwell Brig to lick their wounds and think what to do next!

With the news of the victory came more recruits, boosting the Covenant numbers to near 4,000 men and 2,000 horse. The Duke of Monmouth arrived in person to lead the royal forces, now numbering 15,000. The battle was fought over a bridge, with the rebels having initial success where 300 men were holding the bridge against huge odds. It held for three hours until ammunition ran low. On retreating to the main force the royal cannons pounded the rebels, then sent a large detachment of dragoons among them. The rebels fought well but eventually broke and in the flight from the field 800 were cut down and 1,500 were taken as prisoners. The rebellion was lost. Thousands of covenanter prisoners were herded into Greyfriars cemetery in Edinburgh, where the Covenant was first signed, and in the walled enclosure they were left to starve. Many hundreds were executed. Thousands were deported to the West Indies, and many were abused and killed, treated harshly as named traitors.

As an example, five of the prisoners were selected and marched to Magnus Moor where the archbishop had been murdered, and were hanged on the spot! They had nothing to do with the murder, but examples had to be shown. One of these men was Andrew Gullan, who had actually tried in vain to save the archbishop on the day of his murder.

Today on Magnus Moor five gravestones stand in a ploughed field across from a strange pyramid-shaped stone monolith. The pyramid marks the very spot where the archbishop was murdered and the stones represent the five common men brought as prisoners from Bothwell Brig and mark where they were made an example of and hanged!

David Hackston survived the disaster of Bothwell Brig but was captured after the battle in another skirmish in

Ayrshire where he fought bravely. He was taken in irons to the Edinburgh Tolbooth and sentenced to be hanged with two other Covenanters – Lawrence Hay, a weaver from Fife, and Andrew Pittuloch, a labourer from Largo who had been seen present at an outdoor prayer meeting in the fields behind Largo.

David Hackston was one of the assassins of Archbishop James Sharp. Although he was there and one of the nine, he never laid a hand on the archbishop, but he was sentenced to have first his right hand struck off, then his left, then to be hung by the neck alive and have his bowels slit open and his heart cut out ... while still alive! Afterwards he was to have his head cut off and his body quartered. His head was to be fixed on a spike at Netherbow, one of his quarters with both hands to be fixed at St Andrews, another quarter in Glasgow, the third in Leith and the last in Burntisland.

In July 1681 at the Grassmarket in Edinburgh the two found guilty of nothing more than listening amongst hundreds of others at an illegal out-door protestant preaching in Largo Kirk's boundaries were hanged, then beheaded for it.

The heads of Lawrence Hay and Andrew Pittuloch from Largo were secretly taken from their spikes at the Edinburgh Tolbooth by some kindly friends and buried in Cupar graveyard where also one of the hands of David Hackston was rescued from St Andrews and buried in the same grave. The grave stands in the old kirkyard still, with two heads and a hand carved in the stone. On one side it reads ...

> Our persecutors filld with rage
> Their brutish fury to aswage
> Took heads and hands of martyrs off
> That they might be the peoples scoff

They Hackstons body cut asunder
And set it up a worlds wonder
In several places to proclaim
These monsters gloryd in their shame.

Re-erected July 13th 1792

Of the other murderers of Sharpe, the troops hunting them never got close, but they exacted punishments on the parents of the two brothers Alexander and Andrew Henderson. They were heavily fined – £600. The parents of George Flemming were fined the same. The archbishop's assassins who survived the Drumclog battle lay hidden in the Borders till 1688, when James Russel and George Flemming returned to their own kirks as elders.

Archbishop Sharp was replaced by Archbishop Alexander Burnet, but he would only last till 1688 when William of Orange

The grave of Andrew Pittuloch, David Hackston and Lawrence Hay in Cupar Cemetery

took the British throne and swept away all traces of the Episcopal establishment.

There was talk from Charles II in his day about restoring St Andrews Cathedral, but it came to nothing, and by the end of his reign St Andrews Castle had become a quarry for the building of several nearby houses.

The population of St Andrews was near 15,000 at the turn of the 16th century – by 1700 with plague and war it had fallen to 4,000. The very drinking water drawn from the mill was declared "nasty and unwholesome". Disease raged in the streets, two hundred people dying of a "malignant flux" in a few weeks in 1696. The population continued to leave the dead city. The city now belonged to farmers and fishers, the streets hillocked with dung and rotting fish guts. The once majestic city of learning was a far cry from what it once had been, after the clergy had left it.

Chapter 9

They Sleep with the Fish

In around the year 1100, in the reign of King Alexander I, a wooden pier was constructed in St Andrews for the use of the fishing fleet. Around the Fife coast, towns like Crail, Anstruther, Pittenweem and St Monans all had natural deep-water harbours that required very little maintenance, but the St Andrews harbour, although in a sheltered cove, is very open to the elements, in shallow tidal waters, and full tides are required to enter the safe berths. The first stone pier was constructed in 1559, around the time of the confusion of the Reformation; it was largely built with the stone architecture of the great cathedral. But building materials also available were the ruined remains of the besieged walls of the archbishop's castle that had withstood the abuse of the naval and land bombardment, all were used in the build of the new harbour pier.

An old encyclopaedia says that in 1634 there were 70 fishing boats using the St Andrews harbour. But a huge storm destroyed the pier in 1662. Partly from a collection through the kirks of the area and a donation of £162 from Charles II on his visit here at the same time as the storm, a new sturdy pier was constructed. It was lengthened in 1882 to basically what we see today.

The story of St Andrews fishing fleet is one of misery and utter woe. It's a wonder any fisherman made it to old age, so many and frequent were ships and men lost to this trade. Imagine the hardship in going to sea under nothing but the wind and oars for guidance, with nothing but woollen and leather clothes to keep the bitter North Sea from your bones. Most boats had just a deck, with no room for warmth and protection. The boats still brought back attractive catches. Herring and cod were caught in great numbers, but the cost in human lives was horrendous.

As St Andrews city was created by a shipwreck in 372AD, I follow on to give the tragic history of the St Andrews fishing fleet decade by decade from 1700 to the late 1800s. Many ships would succumb to the same fate as St Andrew's bones, but often with no beach for rescue.

1700–1710

On the 17th of August 1710, seven young St Andrews lads, full of adventure and with casual fishing in mind, left the safety of the stone harbour, rowing with enthusiasm their boat into the North Sea under a clear blue sky, as they had often done before. Soon a swell arose and before they could react, being several miles out from the harbour, they became caught out in a rather ferocious storm. They only carried basic picnic items of food and wine and were totally unprepared for the results of a storm. They were exposed and buffeted about, lost at sea for seven full days, till the boat eventually crashed on a rocky beach near Aberdeen, eighty kilometres up the coast from St Andrews. The boys were so worn out by thirst and fear and want of sleep, that they could scarcely crawl from the beach. The two eldest made the climb up the cliffs to raise help for their friends. A fisherman called Shepherd gave them aid, and medical help came from the local university, but it was much too late for two of the boys who soon died, of exposure and exhaustion.

The oldest of the seven was only fifteen years old. His father was Mr Bruce, a respected man from Edinburgh, who was so grateful for the care Mr Shepherd had bestowed on his son and friends that he gave as thanks a silver plate with an engraved picture of the boys in a boat landing amongst the rocks. The story of the boys and the kindness from the fisherman was big news around the country and many paintings were made on the subject of their ordeal. It is from this disaster that our story of St Andrews fishing fleet starts. And it is one of the early records of fatalities from this harbour.

1760–1770

On 4 November 1765 the little fleet of fishing boats left St Andrews harbour. Then only five small yawls of 8 metres long, they set off with a light breeze, generally getting distance from Dundee into deep waters to fish, using casting lines baited with many hooks, for cod and herring. The herrings came in such vast numbers that they could be caught in nets, tubs, creels, anything at hand, so black were the waters with them. But ominous black shadows skirted the skies, a fierce wind arose and it was obvious to all a storm was brewing. The five ships headed for home but unlike the other deep harbours around Fife, when the tide is out you cannot enter the St Andrews harbour, as the water sits too low. The boat master's choice was to ride out the storm till the tide came in, which could take anything up to six hours, or beach the boats and risk losing them and all the catch of fish.

Wives and friends watched helplessly from the harbour as the boats bravely tried to ride out the storm. People actually waded into the waters with ropes to throw to the stricken crews. Then, in full view of the onlookers, a huge wave lifted by the storm's swell took one of the little ships laden with fish up in the air and smashed it down on top of another boat. The stricken boat's captain had his head split in two from the keel of the dropped boat, blood and brains splattered the deck as he was killed instantly, and the remainder of his crew were thrown overboard as the weight of the dropped boat sank them. Every member of crew aboard the lifted boat had fallen helplessly into the sea, and with all this horror the stricken wives could only watch their men drowning in front of them.

The two boats and cargo were all smashed to pieces. It is a miracle the lower boat's crew – minus the captain – actually survived. Out of the five boats that left the harbour that day only two returned, severely damaged. Twelve men were now dead or drowned.

The loss to St Andrews could be seen as comparatively small in lives lost, but in terms of confidence and commerce it was the entire fishing fleet smashed to pieces and lost in one moment. The wailing of widowed women and the news coming to the taverns made this loss an utter catastrophe. Eleven of the men were married and left widows and children – the people of St Andrews rallied handsomely and found money and support for the stricken families. But the fishing fleet was ruined for the next 35 years. Completely wiped out by this terrible storm, all heart was lost for the risk of fishing.

1800–1810

It took a while but back to the sea men eventually came. The deep North Sea was still hungry for souls, however, and there was many a widow to be made in St Andrews yet!

On 5th January 1800, anyone with ambitions of going back to fishing at sea was given a sharp reminder of the risks, when the sloop *Janet* was driven on to the sands of St Andrews. The ship itself was from Macduff, trying to go up the coast to reach home. Most of the population of the town ran to the beach hoping to aid the ship battling in huge waves 100 metres from the shore. The crew of the stricken boat were exhausted after fighting the storm for many hours; many were resigned to their fate with fatigue, and awaited death from the waves.

A brave young student called John Honey tied a rope round himself and plunged into the sea to swim to the crew's assistance, foolhardy towards his own wellbeing. He managed to swim out and get on board where he seized the men on deck one by one, and manhandled them ashore. They were taken to the Black Bull Inn, where comfort and warmth was eventually provided. The captain of the *Janet* and the five men of the crew were saved by the unselfish, utterly heroic exploits of John Honey. He was to have the freedom of the city bestowed on him in recognition of his unselfish bravery by the Dean of Guild of St Andrews and is commemorated today in many ways.

Three years later in 1803, St Andrews still had no fishing fleet. Fish was coming into the city via the harbours at Crail, Anstruther and Pittenweem. It was suggested by the Dean of Guild Mr Cathcart Dempster, who had an estate in Shetland, to invite fishermen from the Shetlands to bring two boats from Brassey Sound harbour. The deal proposed to the Shetland fishers was to pay each man ten shillings a week, even when the sea was too rough to fish. The deal included paying them some money from the sale of the fish they caught and to sell the fish to St Andrews citizens at a fair price at a barn in Market Street. It was a good deal, thought the fishers from Shetland; before long they appeared in St Andrews' waters with two yawls, using six crewmen in each boat. They were to be called, "The town's fishers".

But the St Andrews lifestyle wasn't for the Shetland men and within two months one ship had left for home again, taking eight of the men. Four men remained and encouraged some local men to come back to the sea with them and trail them as seamen. A fishing trade soon resumed with the one Shetland boat, called the *Craignoon*. Before long, a second, third and fourth boat came to the harbour from the crowded Fife coast ports – St Andrews had a fishing fleet again, albeit a small one.

These boats were of a basic, rude construction, being described at the time as being "as open as mussel shells". Persistent baling out of water consumed a lot of the fishers' time, which I'm sure never convinced any bystanders to follow a life at sea! The general method of fishing was for each man to carry three strings of baited lines 150 fathoms long (a fathom being 1.83 metres) – that makes 275 metres of lines with hooks every 75 centimetres, all baited usually with mussels. Buoys would be floating end to end of the line. It would be thrown in the sea to float for six to twelve hours, then the catch would be picked up and drawn aboard. The caught fish were then thrown into baskets.

With the town investing in its fishing fleet, they safeguarded their assets by having all registered fishermen sign an agreement that if any of them arranged "to deprive the town of the regular take of fish by selling them to cadgers and others at distance" they would be deprived of the privileges of fishermen. Basically this meant loss of payments and use of market and harbour.

In early 19th-century St Andrews, the fish market on Market Street was frowned upon by the growing golfing society. The strong smell and the litter of fish debris, guts and mussel shells did not reflect the ambiance St Andrews upper classes held of themselves. The town provost was held in ridicule for establishing these fishing types, whose children ran wild in bare feet and rags. The living quarters of the fisheries was full of dunghills and untidiness. Posh university society made jest of the hard living fishers, constructing doggerel ...

> One winter night, returning from the club,
>   I brushed my shin against a mussel tub;
> Just at that instant, from the vacant street,
>   A female form rose slowly to its feet;
> An awful odour seemed diffused around,
>   I knew myself on Cloacina's ground –
> The goddess stood before me, all confest.
>   In cast-off duds, like ancient fish-hag dressed!
> Round her coarse neck hung, clattering like bells,
>   A novel necklace formed of mussel shells!
> She smelt of gin like any two Dutch skippers;
>   All down at heel she sported carpet slippers;
> A dirty mutch upon her head she wore;
>   Her hand a besom stick for sceptre bore –
> From a dark cloud a glimpse of moonshine broke,
>   I held my nose, and waited till she spoke!

The author of this ditty is not known but similar comments in prose emanated from the golf society gentlemen, poking fun at the less favoured fishing stock.

While the hard living fishers were the target of abuse, they continued to die catching fish – the fish the golf and university upper classes ate at silver service suppers.

In 1817 another little sloop called the *Packet* sank in high weather just outside the St Andrews harbour. Again it had misjudged the tide and beached on to rocks and sank. Although her crew got off, most of her cargo was ruined.

1820–1830

In 1821 a ship called the *Charles and Agnes*, 45 tonnes, bound for Newcastle with coal, beached itself just outside the harbour and although her crew was saved, the ship was holed and the coal was lost and discharged into the sea.

From 12 January 1823 a huge storm blew almost without intermission till the 24th. Under a cloud of terrible snow, in the darkness, the shadow of a huge ship was seen in difficulty. The *Jean* of Arundel, carrying oak timber beams and 210 tonnes in weight, beached itself smashing itself into pieces. The crew was saved, but for years later the stumps of its hull rose out of the sands at St Andrews.

With the action of the *Jean* on the beach, a kilometre behind her another boat from London the *Itinerant* was also helplessly stranded. She was larger, about 250 tonnes, with 400 tonnes of coal as her cargo. She had left from Newcastle south towards London, but with the storm here she was at St Andrews! The *Itinerant* was beached and the captain and cook were drowned, but a rescue boat manned by St Andrews fishermen saved the rest of the crew.

At the time of the rescue of the surviving *Itinerant* crew a third ship was in difficulty, the *John and Sarah* of Woodbridge also, like the *Itinerant*, loaded with coal. Again its destination was London. A brig of 150 tonnes, she had cast her anchor in the Firth of Tay two days earlier to ride out the storm, but the storm had battered her. Her captain had a choice between letting her sink, or beaching her on rocks and trying to save the cargo. Three men lost their lives and the boat was a total wreck. By the next day all the cargo was lost! ... That was three ships lost in as many hours.

1826 ... A small ship weighing 30 tonnes, the *Friends*, went into difficulty, just north of St Andrews bay. At this time no bridge existed between Fife and Dundee and all trade between the two counties was done by boat. On this instance the ship *Friends* had got into difficulty and was being carried by the waves. The ship took water and sank, but this time her crew were rescued.

There was busy traffic around St Andrews bay, with trading in each direction between Dundee and Newcastle in England. In 1828 the 50-tonne ship *Paragon* left St Andrews harbour laden with ironstone destined for the steelworks in Newcastle. She left the harbour at 2pm in the afternoon and was struck by the *Lavinia* bound for Dundee and laden with coal, about 54 tonnes. The *Paragon* sank immediately with the heavy cargo she was carrying. All her crew managed to jump overboard and were rescued by the *Lavinia*. The *Lavinia* was judged to be at fault and £500 was obliged to be paid from her to the owners of the *Paragon*, a lot of money in those days. The most frightening thing was that this accident had happened in daylight, in reasonable weather.

Another boat in 1829 called the *Peggie*, which was bound for London, got into difficulty, but this time an organised lifeboat full of volunteers from the St Andrews harbour saved the crew. They managed to tow the stricken ship to Dundee harbour, and £80 was given for the ship's rescue.

In 1830, Bob Hutchison, the captain of a creel boat, came to grief after the wind took his sails and toppled the little boat. He was later found drowned.

In November 1831, a Dutch ship stocked with herring barrels set sail from Edinburgh due to reach Hamburg, but outside the Forth Estuary it hit heavy waters and the ship broke up, losing all its cargo on the west sands of St Andrews. Its five crew managed to reach shore but the ship was utterly destroyed.

In May 1833, the *Elizabeth Durham*, a 30-tonne sloop, trafficking in grain, came to grief in St Andrews bay where the Eden River reaches the sea. She was manned by two St Andrews characters, David Morrison and Bob Duncan. Both were seasoned seafarers forty years of age. They left St Andrews and soon the weather had the advantage. The pair fought the storm, but at one point the boat tipped, sending David into the surf. A wooden hold ladder was thrown to him by his friend to keep himself afloat. Alas, it struck him on the head and David Morrison, another of St Andrews' sons, was found washed ashore eight days later by the foot of St Andrews castle; he had a telling wound on his forehead where the ladder had hit. David Morrison was described as a six-foot, strong-built lad, fiery tempered but kind-hearted and a powerful swearer. The *Elizabeth Durham* was sold to a captain in Pittenweem, and the monies raised went to his widow. The ship would come to grief again two years later. Sinking in the Firth of Forth after striking rocks at the Lady's Craig, she lost all her cargo of coals.

In the same storm that David Morrison came to grief in, another of St Andrews' sons was lost on another ship, the

Intellect. The schooner *Intellect*, about 85 tonnes, belonged to the St Andrews coal merchant Mr Robert Pringle, who was an important businessman in the city, his ships trading as far as London and the Baltic region. On its fatal journey it was carrying potatoes as cargo, bound for the city of London, when one of its crew, a James Swan, who was up in the sails, fell to the deck and was killed instantly. Poor James Swan was sewn up in his hammock, given a cannonball as weight and sent to the bottom of the sea just off Bridlington Bay. The *Intellect* would sink off the Danish coast at Elsinore in another storm, with the crew being saved. The captain of this ship, William Pringle (Robert's brother), would send his unlucky crew home on another schooner, he himself taking another boat – which was lost with all hands near the Fern Islands off Northumberland. His remains were washed up near the Berwick coast, very near where he had dropped James Swan to rest in the deep depths.

In 1834, the sloop *Eliza*, coming from Newcastle laden with coal, entering St Andrews harbour collided with another boat, losing all her cargo. The populace managed to retrieve washed-up coal in baskets, and many a St Andrews house was kept warm that winter with the beached fuel. The boat was towed to Dysart and refloated, but was later lost in a storm. It is said the accident would never have happened if the St Andrews pier had been longer.

In 1836, the *Little Jamie*, a small boat, came to grief in the Forth, both Peter Peattie and a young lad David Wood were drowned. Their bodies were washed up on Kirkcaldy beach. It seems the ship's sail caught the wind and toppled the ship.

On 27 June 1838, James Fenton, while in the city of St Andrews celebrating Queen Victoria's imminent coronation, himself a great singer and entertainer, emerged from the taverns the worse for drink and headed out of the St Andrews harbour at three in the morning to bring in his partan creels. His good friend called to his house at five in the morning to report to James his boat had been seen adrift and against the castle of St Andrews. Where James had being laying his creels off St Andrews beach in his drunken state, his weighted creel ropes had caught his leg, entangled it, dragged him from the boat and laid him forever at the bottom of the sea.

In November 1839, an easterly gale brought debris on to the sands at St Andrews. Washed up dead was a large dog, along with several large pieces of timber. It was apparent that another ship had fallen foul of the coastline and weather. It was found to be the *Petrel* from Stockton on Tees, caught in a blinding winter snowstorm. The ship was 400 tonnes, laden with yellow pine logs bound for Grangemouth up the Firth of Forth. She had nine of a crew, who during the gale had set down both anchors to ride out the storm, but they were carried over a deep reef and it tore the ship apart. The crew were all lost bar one. It was noted that the washed up bodies were all smashed by the rolling timbers they were carrying rather than drowned. The only survivor had a badly broken leg but he managed to hold on to one of the wooden spars till he reached the sands and dragged himself ashore. All along the shore was the terrible debris. A pig was washed up alive, but with two broken legs. It was soon taken by the St Andrews folk and dispatched. The captain and his lady passenger were recovered by the next tide, the captain's corpse was tied to a beam, to keep himself from washing overboard in the storm.

In the Kirkyard of Boarhills lies a memorial ...

Residents in this neighbourhood in mournful remembrance of the death of the captain and seven of the crew and a female passenger of the brig "Petrel", of Stockton on Tees with a cargo of timber from Dalhousie North America who were driven upon the rocks below Boar Hills and perished in a dreadful storm on the morning of ... November 1839.

Sufferers' names ...
[name gone] Captain ... From Stockton.
Robert [name lost] First Mate ... Whitby,
Richard [name lost] ... Whitby,
Thomas Lindesay ... Port Glasgow,
John Tate ... Sunderland,
Thomas Watson ... Dumfries,
Samuel Robinson ... New York,
George [name lost] ... Cromar,
Mrs Westcarth ... Richmond Yorkshire

The the only survivor was second mate Henry Thomas from Laugharne in Wales.

The ruins of the *Petrel* were rebuilt by a local merchant on the east of St Andrews, using the timber she had been carrying, but the cursed ship would again sink near here in 1864.

1840–1850

In October 1841, a large brig called the *Riseborough*, about 300 tonnes with 11 crew, was coming from America to dock at St Andrews bay with a cargo of timber. When she beached at the foot of the Boar Hills, all the crew were saved, but the ship being aged smashed itself on the beach. In the same storm a Dunbar sloop laden with coal, the *Jacky Tar*, smashed just before the harbour and it was hard to say which boat was more wrecked, she or the *Riseborough*!

In Autumn 1842, a pretty large topsail-yard sloop, the *Woodyard*, was returning from Newcastle with a general cargo of coal, paint and ironmongery bound for St Andrews. She got too far inshore and grounded on the rocks below the Boar Hills, and the crew got ashore with great difficulty.

At this period up to thirty ships could be using the St Andrews harbour lying at the two little quays. Trade was usually with other British ports and the Baltic regions, in timber, potatoes, slate and grain. Grain was in great demand in London for making gin.

In January 1843 came the foundering of the Leith trader, *St Regulus*. At that time a brisk trade was going on by sea between St Andrews and Leith. The sloop *St Regulus* was about 90 tonnes, her captain was David Peattie and her cargo was wheat, bound for the Edinburgh market. In St Andrews harbour two returning ships made comment to Davie Peattie that he had better rest his sails for the night, as there was a storm brewing and the two harbour-bound ships had had a hard fight to enter the harbour.

But time is money and, eager to impress his bosses, he set out into a hard snow and wicked swell. One of the crew was swept overboard and lost. As the rest battled in vain to keep the craft afloat, she was seen in difficulty around the Fife coast. At Elie she was seen breaking up with only two men on board. In Largo bay she broke up and nothing but a few timbers was ever seen of the boat or her crew ... all gone to the watery depths.

A rare calotype photo taken in the 1840s showing boats in the harbour and the cathedral remains

In October 1844 came the wreck of the *Mary* from South Shields. In a huge storm, "a rolling mass of broken water for miles", the eight crew of the stricken ship made it ashore at St Andrews more dead than alive. The 200-tonne ship was laden with coal and bound for London. Both her anchors snapped and the ship smashed to pieces.

In 1845, the *Po* of Yarmouth grounded in a storm, but after lying dangerously for several tides, enough weight was thrown off her to lift her from the rocks, and she was salvaged.

On 28 January 1848, another huge gale claimed a victim – the *Endeavour* of Maldon came into difficulty six kilometres off St Andrews. Not much was known until four bodies were washed up in St Andrews bay. Her cargo was coal, what exactly caused her problems no one could tell, but the ship broke up under the weather and all perished.

In the cathedral cemetery lies a tablet; chiselled into it reads ...

To the memory of
James Sheldrick
Mariner of Heybridge in the county of Essex, who met his death by drowning in St Andrews's bay, Jan 28th 1848.

That same year a 336-tonne ship called *Horn* ran aground in a dreadful storm. She was already carrying the crew from another wrecked ship, the *Regalia* from Kirkcaldy, which had wrecked itself in Greenland. The whaling ship had sailed throughout the world but close to her home port of Dundee she hit rocks outside St Andrews and went under. All the two crews were saved.

On 10 November 1848 a small crab boat went out to pull in the creels on a lovely morning. On board were two young brothers, one soon to be wed, Henry Duff and his brother Lindsay. The boat was found washed up on the Fife shoreline and the two boys were never seen again. It was nothing but calm, and what happened to the two boys was a total tragedy. Both bodies were claimed by the sea.

In spring 1849, a Prussian barge, the *Johann Frederick*, with a cargo of wheat, hit rocks. The ship was abandoned and the cargo saved but the ship could not be moved and sat on the rocks for over a year and a half till it finally broke up.

1850–1860

At Christmas 1851, the schooner *Hawthorn*, laden with potatoes, left St Andrews in a storm for Newcastle. She set sail because the potatoes were starting to perish with the frost, and she hit terrible weather just outside St Andrews bay and sank with all four of her crew lost.

In 1852, the *Janet Johnstone*, a little sloop carrying a cargo of potatoes bound for Newcastle, set out on a very calm day and much like *Hawthorn* the previous year, a gale blew up, blowing northerly, putting its experienced crew in trouble as the boat took in water. The boat's skipper John Connacher and his mate Davie Hutchison took to baling the water, as the third member of the crew John Sim climbed the mast to free the sails, which were pressing the ship towards danger. Both John Connacher and Davie Hutchison drowned, and the sinking boat broke up, but John Sim held on to the rigging and was washed ashore.

A sad footnote to this latest tragedy from St Andrews harbour fleet was that Captain John Connacher was one of four brothers who were all drowned at sea. John Connacher drowned at Holy Island, one brother at the Farne Islands, one at Stonehaven and another in the Mediterranean. For the mothers and wives of anyone working at sea, it must have been a terrible experience waiting to see the sails of your man's ship across the skyline when his ship was late in ... sometimes never coming!

On 12 July 1853, the *Cybele* was a 200-tonne boat drawing 4 metres of depth in the water, a Dundee ship coming from America. She was too big to get into St Andrews harbour, so was offloaded by boat sitting just off St Andrews bay sands. The annual games were in full swing that day in St Andrews, but the party was stopped with the news that a ship was again on the rocks of St Andrews. The *Cybele* had broken her anchor chains and was hitting the rocks on the bay. The ship was manned by ten crewmen, who managed to get ashore safely, but the ship was mortally wounded and the storm turned her into matchwood. The only saving grace was that they had managed to remove her cargo before destruction.

In March 1857, the *Winterfled*, a Norwegian schooner of 150 tonnes whose cargo was timber from the Baltic, arrived off the St Andrews harbour. Unable to enter the harbour due to the tide being out, she was pulled in close and stuck fast on rocks, where she lay for days unable to float herself away from her doom. A breech was made by the rocks and in rushed the water. Like the *Cybele* before her, her cargo and crew were safe but the boat perished on the rocks. Again St Andrews' tidal-entry-only harbour had claimed another victim.

On 31 March 1858, the *Sutlej* set sail from Dundee. She was a full-rigged ship, one of the largest and smartest sailing from Dundee's dock, carrying 1,200 tonnes with about 35 crew, a ship that had been used by the government at Sebastopol during the recent Crimean War. She had left Dundee with a cargo of timber, iron bedsteads, lining and passengers all bound for Sydney, Australia. The timber was for house construction for miners in the gold rush that had taken over the population there.

She was towed by two tugs down St Andrews bay where she gently struck rocks. No panic prevailed as it was a gentle bump she took, and the tugs released ropes for her sails to unfurl and take the wind. Then water was seen in the compartments; the captain took great alarm at this and started to pump the water back into the sea. The crew panicked and leapt overboard deserting the stricken fully-laden ship. She rode the sea tide into St Andrews bay and at midnight smashed into these famous rocks at St Andrews. Her Sydney-bound goods were pilfered by the local citizens.

On Tuesday 13 April that year another ship hit difficulty. The fishing yawl the *Fox* was seen from the St Andrews shore to be in difficulty – she was sinking! She was rescued by a boat rushing to her assistance and towed into the harbour. She was a Broughty Ferry registered boat 7 metres long belonging to a Mr James Lorrimer. Her crew of five, who had left to go fishing the day before, were all drowned, making one widow and nine children orphans. The dead were named as: James Lorrimer, and three brothers: William, Thomas and James Gall; added to this was James Gall's eighteen-year-old son. The crewmen were recovered along St Andrews beach – one was washed up six months later.

On Thursday 26 May 1858, Mr Craigie, a teller in the Bank of Scotland, left Montrose on his pleasure yacht with five passengers and two crewmen intending to sail to St Andrews harbour. The *Wasp*, which was built for speed, made the journey in fast time and Mr Craigie took his guests for a drink in St Andrews. The boat was sitting just off the harbour – again the tide was out, so no entry could be made. All was fine, with the two seamen left on board as the party made their jollies in the taverns. But there was no understanding of the layout of the harbour, and the tide was still going out! The *Wasp* rested on rocks as the tide gently departed, and soon her weight snapped the hull in two! When the drunken party made their way back from the delights and hospitality of the St Andrews tavern, they were faced by a sunken wreck and two shamefaced sailors.

On Saturday 16 April 1859, with the herring arriving in good numbers, the St Andrews fishing fleet was out and working their lines hard. One fishing yawl the *Feyther* was out in the bay where a schooner going from Newcastle to Dundee blinded by the sun's rays ploughed on ahead, cutting the *Feyther* in two. The boat sank but the crew were rescued. A court case was brought against the master of the *Shardlow* in which the sunken boat got nothing, neither damages nor satisfaction.

On 17 June 1859, the schooner *Galatea* sank six kilometres off St Andrews harbour, laden with coals from Dundee to Newcastle, she sprang a leak in calm waters which could not be stopped. She was so heavily laden she sank, with her masts sticking out the water. No lives were lost.

1860–1870

On 18 February 1861, an unregistered and unknown boat, thought possibly to be from Jersey, grounded herself upon the rocks at St Andrews in a storm, killing four crew. No names of the crew nor name of the boat was found.

On 11 April 1863, Alexander Henderson, a seasoned sailor who had weathered many a rough sea throughout the world, was drowned at the entrance of St Andrews harbour. Alexander could not swim. He fell in while tying his boat up to another. Although a friend got hold of his trouser leg, he could not hold him and the man was lost … his body was found on St Andrews bay two days later.

On 23 October 1864 came the wreck of the *Napoleon*, one of the most heartrending shipwrecks in the bay of St Andrews, which brought shame to the citizens of the city. The brig *Napoleon* stuck on the rocks where many ships before her had come to grief, only this time the citizens of St Andrews stood on the sands 60 metres from the action and did nothing to save the ship or crew – standing inactive watching the drama unfold, with desperate cries from the boat's crew for help!

On Sunday at noon, a large brig under full sail was seen from the shore fighting with one of the biggest storms ever seen at St Andrews. The storm had been blowing for two full days. The *Napoleon* had already lost two of her crew who had fallen overboard. The two first to die were a young boy and an old man. They had drowned and washed up on the beach while the remaining crew still fought for life. A huge crowd stood on Kirk Hill watching the ship in her death throes. The *Napoleon* was carried towards the sands and the crowd followed. On board, the boat's seven crewmen fought valiantly with the rigging, trying to turn the ship seaward again. On the beach the crowd got to within fifty metres of the boat, and a seaman shouting in a foreign accent pointed to the small rowing boats that could be used to help the crew of the floundering ship, but no one understood. The panicking seaman tied a plank and threw it to the St Andrews people with a rope, but no one claimed it. They stood motionless, eyes fixed on the sinking ship. One man held up a board with the words "help is coming", but the seaman again pointed to the boats sitting on the beach. Still there was no action.

By this time the tide was coming in again, causing more destruction upon the boat. The sailor screaming for help had lost the rest of his crew, who had gone overboard and drowned. He stood in the rigging as the ship broke up under him, staring angrily at the motionless people refusing to help him. Then with a last gesture of goodbye he fell into the wild waves. He broke the waves several times bobbing about trying to swim, but exhaustion took him and he disappeared from this life under the waters.

She was the brig *Napoleon* of Uddevalla, a 300-tonne ship heading from Newcastle to Sweden laden with coal.

Seven bodies as well as the first two were collected. Two were found a month later. Some of the bodies were badly cut up; one had half a head, the face and skull smashed in. The seven immediately found were buried at Boar Hills cemetery, the two found a month later were given a burial in the same coffin and interred in St Andrews Cathedral burial ground.

A plaque in the Boar Hills cemetery records the slain Swedish ...

> Henric Odman ... master
> Anton Berntsson ... mate
> Johannes Andersson ... 2nd mate
> Anders Johansson ... carpenter
> Johannes Nilsson ... seaman
> Lars Nilsson ... seaman
> Anton Flink ... seaman
> Johan F. Johansson ... cook
> Charles H. Odman ... son of master

It seems that the waiting people on the beach believed the newly formed St Andrews lifeboat would rescue them, but it never came. What must the stricken boat's crew have thought to see the locals standing inactive, watching as if it was entertainment, not lending a hand where definitely needed.

Many letters made the pages of the *Dundee Advertiser* newspaper, chastising the day's inaction during the tragedy.

Some said "I blush for my native city" or "so scathing to the manhood of our city, other Scottish towns will speak of St Andrews with a hiss, we have the epitaph said 'we did not help them', I would rather fifty St Andrews lives be lost to save these poor foreigners than cower under the

The author standing at an overlook at St Andrews Bay where so many boats were lost

stigma of cowardice", another writer saying "a universal feeling of sorrow for the hapless crew mingled with indignation that every effort was not made to save them!"

Apparently the delay in launching the lifeboat was because the storm was so violent that they presumed the crew of the *Napoleon* doomed already. They thought that if they launched the lifeboat it would itself be smashed to pieces. A request for rocket apparatus was sent to Crail, many hours travel away by horse. That was called for by one in the afternoon and reached St Andrews by 3.45pm. The rockets were launched, carrying ropes at the ship, but all missed. The storm lasted a further three days in its fury, the fiercest experienced in St Andrews' maritime history.

If the death throes of the *Napoleon* brought sadness to St Andrews, sadder still a month later would be the loss of the *Dalhousie*. The *Dalhousie* was an iron-screw steamer. Built in 1861 for trade between Newcastle and Dundee by a firm called the Gourlay Brothers, she was 156 tonnes and 60 horsepower. She was the smallest of the Dundee sea-going steamers and a great favourite with those sailing between the two cities as she was reliable and fast.

She left Newcastle on Wednesday 22 November 1864 at 10am, with fourteen crew and twenty passengers. On board were 172 tonnes of general cargo. The weather was calm when she left, and she was expected to arrive at Dundee by midnight on Thursday.

Nothing is known as to what caused the disaster, but what is certain is that some time on Friday night the *Dalhousie* hit rocks outside the bay of St Andrews. At first wreckage was washed up on the beach, followed by bodies. A gold watch found on a man had stopped at half past twelve. Altogether nine bodies were washed up, all men. The women on board, wearing long dresses as was the fashion, never made it from the ocean's depths, sand it was judged holding the dresses firm at the bottom of the ocean. What did wash up were children's shoes and toys.

Just two days after the *Dalhousie* disaster another ship came to grief in St Andrews bay. The *Sidonia*, a Prussian barque, was lost. The newspaper, the *Advertiser* stated:

The wreck of a large vessel supposed to be the Dalhousie was seen from St Andrews yesterday morning. She is all under water but her masts, on one of which a sail is still set. There was some talk of sending out the lifeboat but it was said small boats had been to her and no further effort was needed. At noon a large barque was seen in the bay, with a signal of distress flying at her main. Her cargo or ballast seemed to have shifted, as she was almost on her beam ends. Several parties who knew said they were signalling for help. The lifeboat crew refused to go off saying there was no necessity – the coxswain being backed by most of the committee present. After being in the bay with the signal flying for five hours she stood out to sea, and by night disappeared out of sight.

All fourteen crew were saved, except for the cabin boy, who went down with the boat ... his body was never recovered.

Again public anger filled the newspapers as once more it seemed St Andrews had watched as another boat had sunk in front of her.

On 5 January 1865, came the loss of the *Andrew Wilson*, a schooner of 95 tonnes laden with pit props, destined for Newcastle from the Moray Firth. The ship had holed and was taking in water when a rescue ship came alongside looking for salvage and a prize to take to the harbour. Another ship turned up demanding salvage rights as well – one captain brandished a metal spike threatening "to smash in skulls" if the other boat did not leave. In the middle of the argument, the *Andrew Wilson* sank, taking with her one of her crew, a lad of 19 years called Andrew Gourlay.

In April 1865, a fishing yawl capsized. "Billy the boy" was drowned (otherwise known as William Thomson, a man of 60) with Henry Waters and Jamie Wilson. A sudden gust of wind overturned the boat laden with fishing creels. Billy was found drowned still holding on to two floating bladders. Billy was in the habit of getting violently drunk and squaring up to people in the street in nothing but shorts wanting a fight! He got his nickname for loudly swearing that "he was Billy the boy". He was a great character of St Andrews and the three were much grieved over.

On 17 October 1865, a schooner was seen off the coast of St Andrews fighting its way through a storm with all sails up. Her skipper was fighting a losing battle – the *Fear Not* went over the remains of the *Dalhousie*, either hit the ship or the rocks that had destroyed that proud ship. The *Fear Not* struck both her anchors as her crew battled for life, and the St Andrews lifeboat was launched, dragged to the beach by three plough horses and a cheering crowd. But the storm was so strong that the lifeboat found itself blown back to the beach by the wicked storm.

That night the lifeboat tried again: it was as stormy as before but with the reputation of the St Andrews people already under question, with the disasters and embarrassment of the two ships *Napoleon* and *Dalhousie*, this time – brave as lions – the lifeboat volunteers reached the stricken ship. The captain, the mate, his son and wife were taken off more dead than alive. One man of nineteen was a casualty, found lying in a heap of ropes. He had died from exposure, his body was still warm and the boat just a few minutes too late. The boat was 24 years old, built in Boston, England. After the storm had abated, her hull was found not to be so damaged, and was dragged to Tayport where she was repaired and refloated for £400. She was sold and worked for another twenty years till she broke up on the rocks of Inverkeithing – she sits now at the bottom of the Firth of Forth.

On Saturday 5 January 1867, the brig *James Chadwick* left Montrose heading towards Seaham just south of Sunderland, travelling in fine weather. In the darkness she supposedly ran into trouble and they dropped anchor, waiting for the light of day to get their bearings and continue south. At 3am the chain for the anchor snapped and the boat drifted into the rocks. The captain set fire to two tar barrels to attract attention from the shore and hopefully the lifeboat crew. No movement came from the shore and about 8am the waters had calmed enough to exit the ship and take all belongings with them – including a canary in a cage!

The waterlogged crew took themselves to the very posh Golf Hotel to announce their woes – a stiff glass of whisky and warm clothes were provided. But the amount of possessions they carried indicated that no panic had taken over as the ship went down. The other wrecks had produced exhausted survivors grateful for a warm glass, but there was something relaxed and too casual about this latest bunch of survivors. On inspection of the *James Chadwick*, it was found that all the wooden hatches below deck had been removed, allowing the ship to take on water and sink. It seemed the ship's owners had decided to scuttle her and make it look like a drama – another sea tragedy at a recognized black spot. Her normal trading was between London and Aberdeen, but steam-powered ships had superseded her in speed and reliability. The insurance never paid up and the remains of the broken ship were sold for £8. It was ransacked and the hull, spars, ropes and sails were taken, leaving the wooden spars sticking out of the sands. They could still be seen in 1883 and were regarded as a hazard for fishers.

On 4 May 1867, the *Pilot*, a small schooner, ran into difficulty and its crew was rescued by the lifeboat from St Andrews. On the 20th another small boat was rescued, the *William and John*. Both boats were lost, but their crews were saved.

On 6 December 1867, the *Christian and Charlotte*, a 23-tonne sloop carrying a valuable cargo of wine and fruits assessed at £1,000, was travelling from Leith to Peterhead when it ran aground. The crew and cargo were saved but the ship broke up on rocks.

On 24 January 1868, came the total wreck of the foreign brig *Duopartes*. This brig, being 123 tonnes, carrying bones, was smashed to bits on the Eden river, all crew were successfully rescued.

On 19 September 1868, the foreign brig *Oscar* was wrecked. She was a huge ship, 199-tonnes loaded with heavy batons, coming to Dundee from Sandesund in Norway. About midnight on Friday 18th, a sudden east-north-east gale set in, with tremendous unrest. Showers of sleet and rain continued into the Saturday. On the St Andrews horizon, a ship was seen about 8 kilometres west. The lifeboat was launched with her crew of volunteers, and reached the stricken boat with difficulty in the huge swell: all eight of the crew were rescued. The ship smashed itself on to the rocks.

The conditions were the worst ever seen and the bravery showed by the lifeboat crew was not forgotten. The *Advertiser* wrote...

> St Andrews people think that Saturday's storm was even more severe than the one that drove the "Napoleon" ashore with such terrible results, and that the lifeboat went off in a wilder sea that raged on that deplorable day. All honour to the brave fellows who faced the storm

It seems one of the lifeboat team was hesitant to go, but he was pushed aside, with another bystander getting into the boat in his place, so eager was he to wipe away the blemish of cowardice that had hung over them since the *Napoleon* disaster. Poems were written to mark the bravery shown and were hailed around the taverns of St Andrews. Below is an extract of an anonymous poet's writings:

> "For honour! Now for God's sake try!"
>   The crowd deep murmured, standing by,
> "We'll do our best!" the crew then cried,
>   And nobly they the rescue tried.
> "What though the breakers round us roar!
>   We've braved such seas, such storms before!
> We will now try that crew to save,
>   Although we fill a hero's grave;
> We cannot stay while others steer,
>   To brand us with a coward's fear!"

On 29 November 1868, the smack *Canton* of Scarborough was full of herrings destined for Leith docks when she came into difficulty. The St Andrews lifeboat rescued the crew, and pulled the ship into the harbour for safety.

On 30 September 1896, the Norwegian schooner *Risobank*, an iron-hulled boat built in Inverkeithing in 1868, was 186 tonnes filled with empty casks and 12 tonnes of paraffin oil. She seemed overloaded, stuck on sands and was towed to Leith to be repaired.

1870–1880

On 21 October 1870, Willie Wilson, a St Andrews fisherman, drowned. While rescuing the Danish schooner *Let*, which had mistaken the Eden river for the Tay and the entrance to Dundee where she was to dock. She beached on the sands, several boats were discharged to pull her free when Willie Wilson and others fell into the sea, it was recorded as a misadventure, as Willie and others were seen to be "making fun" when the boat, being top heavy with men, overturned.

In 1871, William Chisholm died on board the schooner *Philomel*, at 57 years old, just landed at St Andrews harbour, due to a chest infection.

On 13 February 1871, a fisherman drowned from the *Express*, one of the harbour's fishing fleet. When coming in view of the harbour, David Brown leant over to remove a buoy floating near. He fell in head first and drowned. Only 18 years old, his body was never found.

On 24 August 1871, a Dundee ship, the *Osprey*, came into difficulty 5 kilometres from the pier at St Andrews. At midnight rockets were seen, distress signals from the ship, it was evident she was going down fast. Nothing was found. Two days later, bodies were washed up. The skipper was to be married, as his body carried a gold ring in its box! Six others of the crew were never found.

On 4 April 1875, the *Catherine Boland*, 99 tonnes, was wrecked on the same rocks that had claimed the *Napoleon*. A hard oak schooner, she was totally destroyed, but crew were saved.

On 21 May 1875, the schooner *Iola* foundered after coming from Sunderland with cement for the building of the first Tay Bridge. She struck rocks and her hold was last seen one and a half metres deep in water. The *Iola* sank in five fathoms of water (9 metres) and was a hazard to the fishing fleet for years.

On 27 May 1875, the *Union* left Crail with ballast due for the Tay Bridge, sprang a leak in the engine room and ran ashore in St Andrews bay – all the crew were saved.

On 13 October 1875, Willie Cargill, fisherman, drowned. He fell overboard fighting a storm coming into St Andrews Bay in a 12-metre boat. His body was never recovered, but he was hailed as "one of the best steersmen in the North".

On 18 October 1875, the wreck of the *Leopold*: the St Andrews lifeboat was launched towards this stricken ship in a heroic rescue that redeemed the reputation of the lifeboat crew, the local *Advertiser* giving praise:

The St Andrews lifeboat has redeemed its character by an act of real heroism; the sail through the wild St Andrews surf was that of brave men, there was readiness and discipline to wipe out old scores. The St Andrews life boat is now manned not by lily livered brawlers but by a crew before whom it is an honest joy to clap one's hands, well done.

On 20 October 1875, came the total wreck of the German barque *Fantee*. Two days after the *Leopold* another ship smashed into the rocks. The *Fantee* was 264 tonnes with a crew of nine. At the first signs that she was in difficulty the lifeboat was launched, but due to the storm the boat could not get off the beach no matter how they tried. The *Fantee* was dragging both her anchors across the bay towards the rocks at the foot of the castle. The crew all managed to escape and the next tide lifted her on to the rocks causing devastation.

On 28 April 1876, the wreck of the *Duncan Dunbar*. This schooner was 62 tonnes, full of coal, heading from the Tyne to Dundee with three old men on board. She had sprung a leak and was taking on water fast. The lifeboat saved the men but the ship collapsed in on itself at the mouth of the harbour and lost all its cargo.

Finally in 1876 a decision was made to deepen the harbour, simply because 15 vessels were stuck at the upper harbour full of grain and potatoes which were perishable items. The boats were stuck, losing money on wages and wasted goods while marooned in the harbour waiting for a decent tide to launch them to sea. Some had been sitting for nine weeks! It was seen as undeniable that the reason for so much disaster was the tidal nature of the harbour, with a decision to deepen the harbour being long overdue. A quicker decision on this would have saved so many lives.

1880–1890

On 22 April 1880, a young man drowned from a rowing skiff. It was a holiday in St Andrews, and Robert Porter decided to test his new boat, but it led to disaster. Taking on water in the bay, his boat was swamped, and although he clung on to the hull, he slipped into the water, never to be seen again.

On 5 March 1881, through the haze of a wicked storm another ship was seen in difficulty. The *Merlin* was a barque; she was completely at the mercy of the storm "as powerless as a cork". She struck rocks 300 metres from the castle ruins, within 15 minutes she was smashed to matchwood, and bodies were soon found on the beach. The boat was carrying coal and it was now scattered all over the beach, turning it black. Men were seen struggling in the waves, but one by one they disappeared under the waves. There was nothing anyone could do, rockets with ropes had been fired at the ship, but it couldn't help what was happening. Only four of the eleven crew's bodies were found.

The dead were named:

Captain Griffith Lewis ... aged 41 ... his body was found and returned to Sunderland for burial.

J. G. Brown ... 28

W. Carty ... 24

Benjamin Pitt ... 64

C. Coulston ... 20

John Neal ... 26

Cuthbert Dixon ... 24 ... his body was found wedged in rocks – it took ten men to free it.

S. Rowe ... 18 ... his body was found.

Charles Swinney ... 19

R. Hetherington ... 19

Lynn Klaas Post ... 39

The three sailors found were buried in St Andrews cemetery. This storm was so fierce and destructive to shipping, that no fewer than 30 vessels came to grief around the coastline of Scotland, with over 200 casualties being drowned between Wick and North Carr!

Chapter 10

The Rabbit War of 1801–21

The town of St Andrews is no stranger to Scotland's many battles and disputes, whether at home or abroad. William Wallace took and destroyed the castle here when held by the English in 1296, and in 1336 Andrew Moray again bashed the English garrison that had retaken it from Wallace and destroyed it. In 1429 the Provost, Hugh Kennedy, took an army from St Andrews to fight with Joan of Arc in France.

John Knox was one of the dissenters who assaulted the castle and held it for a year till French troops blew it apart with cannon fire. General Montrose schooled here and excelled in his archery, winning titles in St Andrews' competitions before carving himself into the history books with his military exploits, crushing his parliamentary enemies in battles the length of Scotland for his king's cause.

One dispute is relatively forgotten, but does deserve a mention in this book, not just for the length of the argument but because it reached the very heart of Parliament to resolve it – the conflict became very violent and split society once again in the town. Mention the town of St Andrews today, and the first reaction will probably

On the alert

be: "Ah yes, the home of golf," with golf being "The Old Course", the famed, 18-hole, picture-postcard tourist attraction and landmark which the town is so famous for. But back in 1800 the 18-hole course had a few extra holes in it ... 895 to be precise!

The story starts in February 1797. The town was in an awful state of near bankruptcy, and desperately needed cash from somewhere to keep itself afloat. The town baillies managed to persuade two rich merchants John Gunn and Robert Gourley to advance the town £2,080 sterling. As security against the loan the council formed a bond over the Links course that gave the merchants the right to sell it if needed at public auction.

Seeing a great opportunity to cash in, they did just that! In November 1797 they sold part of it to to Thomas Erskine for £805.

In 1799 Erskine in turn sold the right to use the land for an annual payment to Charles Dempster and his son.

The Dempsters rented the land for £130 a year to James Begbie who bred rabbits, selling the pelts and meat to local butchers. It is here that the arguments started. For the golfers who used the course it was a nightmare – before long the rabbit population living on the course links was huge, and rabbits love to dig warrens full of holes! The golfers now had hundreds of holes for their balls to drop into instead of the regulated 18.

The bunnies bred like (ahem) BUNNIES! There were thousands of them and the upper-crust golfers could stomach no more of the invasion, so finally decided something had to be done to save their sport. The new club captain, Hugh Cleghorn, led the complaint against the rabbit invasion. A committee was created to sue the Dempsters and campaign against the rabbits. With the rich elite in the clubhouse, funds came quickly and in no time £1,000 was available to fight the Dempsters in court! The battle lines were drawn and both sides now man-oeuvred their forces against each other to fight it out in court.

The day came. The golfers pointed out to the magis-trates that citizens had enjoyed the uninterrupted privilege of playing golf for over 200 years, and now it was threatened. They wanted the course protected from the damage it had suffered, and protected against the tenants' desire to use it as a rabbit warren. They demanded that the Dempsters remove the rabbits and preserve the course. Many witnesses were brought forward to give the motion strength.

It was said that the green keeper, Charles Robertson, had resigned because he could not keep up with the rabbit repairs. A golf-playing witness, George Mitchell, came forward to say he shot into a rabbit hole "three holes running" during a game.

The court was informed that 895 holes had been made by the rabbits on the course; between the 7th and 8th holes 232 rabbit holes were registered.

Naturally the Dempster family said that the course was perfectly playable, but the court in May 1806 decided that the golfers had the right to destroy the rabbits and the defendant had a responsibility to see that no damage was done to the golf course.

A victory was celebrated by the golfers, but the battle was only starting ... a couple of months later the furious Cathcart Dempster (Charles's son) published an advertisement, that read ...

To the inhabitants of St Andrews

You have been stimulated by unsigned advertisements in the name of the Magistrates and Golfers, to destroy the private property of my father and I on the links of St Andrews, on the ground that you had an undoubted and legal right to do so, but I would advise you to pause, before you venture to act upon such vague authority. Far be it for me, to encroach upon any of your lawful privileges, but killing of rabbits on these Links is NOT one of them!

The Dempsters had found old records allowing William Gib to put his black and white rabbits on the Links "during the Council's pleasure" in 1726. Dempster argued that when the Council granted his father and him a "disposition" to the links, they were already under a lease of 19 years as a rabbit warren, granted by the present Chief Magistrate and the Town Clerk.

But an attempt to persuade the courts to prevent the golfers shooting the rabbits failed.

To the golf club members' dismay, Dempster now started building a little dyke – a wall – across the course between the 3rd and 4th holes.

In 1807 John Fraser, a golf club member, was violently attacked by the Dempsters' men. Hostilities continued for the next few years till eventually in 1812 the matter went to appeal in the House of Lords in Westminster. After four days, Lord Eldon, the Newcastle-born Lord Chancellor, found inconsistencies in the decisions of the lower court.

He dismissed the finding that the golfers had the right to destroy the rabbits, and said that the Council had no rights whatsoever over the golf course, so long as feu duty was paid. Lord Eldon even suggested that the golfers were lucky they did not have to contend with cowpats on the course. The matter was referred back to Scotland's Court of Session.

Peace finally came in 1821 … when James Cheape, a wealthy landowner, bought the links land outright. He happened to have a farm not far from the links that was being devoured by the plague of rabbits; a witness had estimated 900 bunnies were living on the course and they were treating his farm like a restaurant. Cheape's purchase ended the St Andrews rabbit war, but he died soon afterwards, in 1824.

His grandson James went on to sell the golf course to the Royal and Ancient in 1894. Would you believe – in his final business accounts it was found he did business with the St Andrews butcher Robert Pratt … selling rabbit meat!

Chapter 11

First World War VC – John Ripley

On 14 August 1933 it was an overcast day with sporadic little rain showers in St Andrews, and a slight breeze, but nothing to stop people going about their way.

The High Street was still busy with the left-over tourism of last month's 68th Open Golf Tournament. In the newspapers much was being made of a strange sighting at Loch Ness in the Highlands. Mr George Spicer and his wife, while driving around the loch, had nearly run into a massive, beast-like, marine creature. It had been so startled by the car it had panicked, crushing the undergrowth flat to reach the waters of Loch Ness. Within a month there was another sighting and this time there was a photo for evidence. The beginning of a legend!

On a roof in St Andrews as a legend formed upon the misty Loch of Ness, another Highland Scottish legend was about to call time on his amazing life! Sixty-six-year-old John Ripley was up on a house roof, removing the old slate carefully layer by layer, with a pallet nearby full of replacements. He stepped off the roof on to the wet wooden ladder leading to the ground – the ladder gave way. John fell heavily and would be pronounced dead at the St Andrews Memorial Cottage Hospital within the hour.

John had been born on 20th August 1867 in Banffshire in the Highlands. As a man he found employment scarce in the Highlands, and so he ended up living in St Andrews as a slater and general roofer, until the call came for soldiers, as the warring factions started to tear French soil apart with the opening salvos of what would be World War One.

John enlisted in the Black Watch Regiment 1st Battalion.

It was May 1915 and the French Commander-in-Chief, General Joffre, asked the British Expeditionary Force to help in an immediate push against German lines north of Arras. The plan was to break through the enemy lines with help from the French Tenth Army. The French objectives were to seize the heights at Vimy Ridge, with an attack at nearby Carency and Roclincourt to capture the heights of Notre Dame. The British assault at "Aubers Ridge" was to commence the day after the French attack and was to be managed by Sir Douglas Haig.

Heavy rain postponed the original French assault on 6th and 7th May, but with the thousands of men stationary and up to their knees in mud, it was 48 hours of endurance until in desperation on the 9th the chiefs ordered the attack, and now it was to commence in unison. The previous orders of the 24-hour staggered assault had been overruled.

The land the British units had to cross was remarkably flat, and occasional drainage ditches cut across the area, some too wide to jump over (4.5 metres). With little covering ground and the water obstacles, it was clear the Germans trenches 450 metres away had a magnificent view of an open killing ground. The Germans in their positions holding the ridge that the British were expected to take had a high, downward view of the field. It was obvious to all but General Haig that this assault would be costly.

The French attack was to be supported by the artillery of the West Riding Division. The French believed short artillery barrages to be ineffective, so they opened up a two-day, methodical, slow barrage, trading surprise for sheer weight of shelling. General Haig did not adopt the same strategy for the British, deciding instead to go for a short initial 40-minute bombardment, followed by the land forces' attack. Around five hundred heavy guns opened the bombardment.

The open ground was strung out with barbed wire; the German positions included machine-gun nests every 20 metres protected by thick steel plate. Arial observations had reported that the German positions had recently been recently strengthened.

The British assault was led by I Corps (1st and 47th Divisions), IV Corps (7th and 8th Divisions) and the Indian Corps (3rd and 7th Divisions).

At 5am the British bombardment started. The French bombardment had been constant for the last forty-eight hours; it could be heard in the distance as the British waited in trenches packed with equipment and men.

At 5.30 the heavy guns switched from shrapnel to high explosives as the lead assaulting brigades of 1st Division finally went over the top ... heavy machine-gun fire now came from the German positions. The British fell in heaps as the bullets found easy targets of hundreds of bunched men. It was simple to just mow the men down, even from their own ladders.

The advancing men, urged on by their officers, soon struggled to advance over the growing heap of their own dead! The Indian Corps couldn't get a man over their own parapet; everyone shot back into the trench, riddled by machine-gun bullets as the trench filled up with bloody corpses.

The British barrage ended at 5.40 and the Seaforth Highlanders joined the attack, suffering the same fate as the Indians.

What few men did make it past the killing zones of the trench rim were now mercilessly shot down on the flat ground by machine-gun nests that lay hidden and unseen at ground

Corpl. JOHN RIPLEY, V.C.

John Ripley portrayed on a cigarette card

level. Whole lines of men leapt in the air, cut in half by the hail of bullets and dead before they touched the ground.

By 6am the attack had failed, all objectives lost. However command ordered a further bombardment at 6.15am and the attack to commence again as before. At this point Major General Harking, CO of 1st Division, offered his opinion that the attack was a failure, which resulted in a further hour and a half of bombardment.

By first light at 8am Haig received the disappointing report on the morning's push so far, and he resolved to renew the effort with a further barrage at 2pm and a further assault.

By this time it was seen that the Germans had just reinforced their positions, yet again a further bombardment was ordered by Haig.

By 3.57 the Black Watch had been brought in to replace the shattered 2nd Brigade. They launched themselves at the

German positions just as the British bombardment stopped. They suffered enormous casualties. The South Wales Borderers and 1st Gloucestershire regiments were in support, but during the attack they were mown down in hundreds ... They didn't reach the enemy lines.

At this point in the battle 47-year-old Corporal John Ripley with the Black Watch had managed by luck to get beyond the hail of bullets and reach the German positions. What was left of his company was seven men!

John was first man into the trench where he established command over his men, and directed fire upon the German defenders. He advanced to the second line of trenches (which was the day's objective), where German reserves now fired upon his position.

John stayed and returned fire until all seven men with him were killed. He himself took a sore head wound and now had no option but to abandon the position and return to his own trench. At this moment further regiments were thrown forward as John retreated. In this confusion, as the King's Royal Rifle Corps were being mown down by machine guns only yards from their own lines, John actually made his way through the carnage back to his own position.

By nine that night it was realised that the artillery barrage had suffered from defective fuses which had not exploded when the shells had hit the wet muddy ground ... the German defences were relatively untouched.

More than 11,000 British casualties were taken on the 9th May assaulting the ridge at Aubers. It was one of the worst rates of loss in the entire war; nothing was achieved by the British assault. Although the French did break through the German lines, the Germans recovered, and in weeks overcame what was lost.

The Black Watch lost 883 men of which 29 were officers. In General Haig's private papers we learn that two days later he stated, "The defences in our front are so carefully and so strongly made ... that in order to demolish them a *long methodical bombardment* will be necessary", but that was after the event.

There is no memorial to "Aubers Ridge". The battle was a complete disaster.

My grandfather George Mason (born in St Andrews) was in the vicinity of this battle with a heavy artillery unit. He survived the Great War. For the author to go to nearby Dundee premier football grounds and see 10 to 11,000 fans in the ground ... it's a sobering thought that this was the amount of casualties on a single day.

John Ripley, who was one of the few to actually achieve (at least for a while) the day's objective, was awarded the Victoria Cross. It was presented to him on 12 July 1915 by King George V at Buckingham Palace. He was made Sergeant of 3rd Battalion Royal Regiment of Scotland. His Victoria Cross was the 613th issued. He was made a Freeman of St Andrews for his achievements and lived there till his accident in 1933. For the horrors he witnessed alone in this fight his VC was utterly deserved.

After his death John Ripley was buried with full military honours.

He has a headstone in Upper Largo cemetery; his grave was re-dedicated in 2001.

Chapter 12

Nazi Bombs Fall on St Andrews

It was 1942 in St Andrews. War had lasted three years, and in Europe Britain was now fighting the Nazi menace alone. France, Poland, Denmark, Holland, Norway and Belgium had all fallen and although Hitler had invaded Russia the year before, he had not given up on Britain.

The Forth Railway Bridge had been attacked early in the war. In Fife air raids became more frequent after the collapse of Norway and Denmark as the Germans could use the Norwegian airfields to attack targets such as Methil and Rosyth dockyards – where Britain's North Atlantic fleet lay in shelter.

The Clyde dockyards and Glasgow were targeted and many hundreds died as they carpet-bombed industrial areas. For the German pilots, that was no picnic, it was a hellish mission, outlasting the fuel reserves of their fighter planes, the bombers went on alone, sometimes having as little as ten minutes' air space over the Clyde to jettison the deadly payload and make for home on minimal fuel.

The RAF fighters based at Drem in East Lothian and Turnhouse near Edinburgh would have the first bite when the enemy was sighted. Gun emplacements on Inchcolm island and along the Forth coastline would give the slow German bombers a hostile reception (my medieval tower in Pittenweem still has Bren Gun fixings on the parapet roof, it has a 30m height and a view over the Forth). And when the Spitfires joined the chase the German bomber gun crews would have a hot time of it.

Sometimes the reception was too hot and the German Luftwaffe, suffering terrible casualties, turned about for home without reaching their deadly payload's destination, releasing the bombs anywhere just to lose the weight they carried and escape the British fighters.

On 6 August 1942, at half past eleven at night a strange but horrible sound wailed around the quiet streets of St Andrews. Rising and falling, it was the haunting moan of the air raid sirens!

The procedure was for people to head to their own house cellars or downstairs hallways and await the continuous sound of the "all clear" signal from the sirens. There was nothing substantial in St Andrews to interest the Nazis, so it was assumed to be a regular raid on the west coast, with the German planes travelling across St Andrews for other targets. Nothing to worry about really, just a massive inconvenience.

William Stewart was the St Andrews Fire Service engine driver. The trouble was that his fire engine was down at the harbour and very exposed. The air raid siren went off, and he started the truck to drive it back to the fire station at Bridge Street and await further orders. On the journey there was a complete blackout. No lights showed, or they would illuminate the town and help enemy planes to get their bearings. So the fire truck was driving near blind towards its headquarters, when all of a sudden the truck was thrown backwards in a violent eruption turning night into day!

The fire truck in St Andrews during the Second World War

The fire truck was just pulling into the station drive when the explosion took out a couple of houses on Nelson Street. A massive piece of shrapnel had gone through the fire station doors, exactly where a few seconds later the fire engine driven by Willie Stewart would have parked. There was chaos everywhere, flames and destruction rained around William as he fought to escape his fiery hell around him.

Perhaps the pilot of the German bomber had failed on a mission to bomb a target further west, had turned about, released his bombs and set out for home. With the blackout he may have had no idea the town of St Andrews was below. Or it could have been one of the east coast 'tip and run' raids. I would like to think this was a dreadful mistake by the pilot and not a calculated attack on a civilian target ... but we will never know for sure.

*

A family on holiday from Lanark were in "Dunusan", one of the houses: John and Margaret MacDonald, both 48, with children Mary and Dorothy.

The preliminary report stated that bombs were dropped in behind Bridge Street and nearby Nelson Street and Park Street. Three were dead, three injured and two were trapped.

The all clear signal was given at 23.44 hours, but the damage left was shocking. Fourteen people were killed, including all four of the MacDonalds from Lanark. They were buried at Roundel cemetery in St Andrews, where Union Jacks were put across the graves.

Devastation in Nelson Street

Chapter 13

The St Andrews Sausage Slaughter

It was Saturday 16 January 1943, and Claude Arthur Cuthbert was standing in his pyjamas looking at his front door. He pulled the edges of his moustache as the grandfather clock in the hallway struck eight o'clock. Paper boy late once again, he thought, and let out a despairing sigh! He went to the larder cupboard in the kitchen, and saw the huge chunk of cheese he had taken from the stores at the Observer Corps station. Being an officer does have its perks, he thought. The lump of cheese was about four times what a weekly ration would be – the rations imposed as the War dragged on.

It was now over three years since Hitler had invaded Poland and another world war had erupted and all were suffering from the madness of it. The convoys of merchant navy ships from America were being systematically targeted in a bid to starve Britain into surrender. The German U-boats were having success, many ships going to a watery grave, and Britain was now rationing the food it had.

Claude's wife appeared from the outside privy, carrying a bucket of coal and with the newspaper in her hand. "Ha!" exclaimed Claude with a laugh. "There's me standing cursing the paper boy and you have it all along."

"Oh, he's on his bike going through Wardlaw Gardens. He handed it to me over the wall as he saw me in the garden," said his wife, handing the paper to her husband.

Claude sat at the kitchen table, opened the paper and spread it over the white tablecloth. His wife went into the pantry cupboard and brought out some waxen parcels in brown paper tied up with string. "I could do sausage and cheese rolls for breakfast, my dear, if you fancy?"

Claude mumbled a "Yes, oh yes" while skimming across the headlines of the newspaper. The Soviets were defending the city of Stalingrad and finally having the best of it on that bloody battlefield; in big letters it read "Royal Air Force bombs Berlin", and it seemed Charlie Chaplin the movie star comedian was making his own news, creating a scandal by dating Oona O'Neill, a 17-year-old girl. He was nearly 55!

Claude carried on reading, and the lovely smell of pan-fried sausages filled the kitchen as his wife busied herself over the cooker. Claude's dog lay in his bed, obedient and waiting patiently, knowing his own breakfast would be soon. But half an hour after breakfast Claude would go to the outside privy, and be violently ill. It would soon worsen. "Were those sausages off?" he cried to his wife.

"No, not at all – fresh from James Martin's butchers just yesterday."

Claude was staggering. "I'm not right – God, I feel ill!" When his wife picked up the remaining linked sausages and sniffed them, there was no obvious bad smell to them. They had been tasty enough, she thought, and freshly made just on the Friday morning, but even so there was also an ominous feeling in her own stomach now. She had eaten a bread roll and sausage with her husband! She picked up three links of pork sausage and gave them to the dog. He wagged his tail and he took the booty to his wooden bed by the stove.

All over St Andrews the breakfast scene above would be mirrored – families tucking into their usual fare, university students reading the daily papers, maids and wives cleaning out fireplaces, and making breakfasts, men getting ready for work. Many within hours of eating would be vomiting and suffering the most awful stomach pains. Within twenty-four hours Claude Arthur Cuthbert would be dead. Others would also die, and at least 150 St Andrews citizens would be absent from work duties ... poisoned by arsenic!

Arsenic is a heavy metal that exists in compound forms, it causes severe gastroenteritis, hypersalivation and major organ failure, vomiting and respiratory distress. In the right dose it can be fatal, and it is usually used for pest control ... and also as a weapon of murder!

Dr Norman McCloud and Dr Redford Taylor being the two resident doctors in St Andrews now had their surgeries swamped with ill citizens, and more were being helped to hospital. They came to the conclusion that the symptoms of the distress mirrored what one would expect as the results of arsenic poisoning! It seemed all had eaten sausages from James Martin and Sons, the local butchers at 2 Church Street.

Samples were taken from Mr Cuthbert's sausages and tested in the laboratories and found to have 1.4% arsenic in them, white arsenous oxide, or 102.2 grains per pound. A fatal dose!

Another victim Miss Susan Garland from 15 South Street had also died she had 1.4% or 98 grains per pound in her sausages, again bought from Martin's the butchers.

John Martin from East Grange farm in St Andrews had run the butchers at 2 Church Street for over forty-five years. Some of his own family had fallen with the illness as well, but it was a complete mystery to him as to where the arsenic had come from. Who could have tipped it into the sausage meat the day before?

On Friday Martin himself was absent, being ill at home, but he telephoned the shop to make sure the sausage meat was being properly prepared and made. He did mention that the meat may have been over seasoned, and even requested that the sausages should be withdrawn from sale!

A full investigation was carried out and in court on 5 April Mr Martin was asked by the fiscal, Mr R S Henderson whether arsenic was kept in the shop.

He answered, "No," and when asked, "Are you bothered by rats?" he answered, "Yes, but I only use traps or cats to get rid of them."

"Are there any poisons laid down?"

Again he answered, "No."

The whole case was deemed a mystery. The meat Martin had asked to be withdrawn had been secretly dumped on the sands of St Andrews, and was fetched to the police for evidence the next day, when the shop was investigated. But three more batches of sausage were produced from the shop on Friday 15 January. One batch had been delivered to the University students at St Salvator's Hall, where they were eaten for lunch by the hungry students in the form of "toad in the hole". Afterwards 90 students became seriously ill. What adds to the mystery is that since 1851 under the Arsenic Act all sales of arsenic were monitored and recorded, and could only be made if the vendor knew the buyer personally. So where had the arsenic come from?

Sheriff Mr More summed up that it was very clear that Mr Cuthbert and Miss Ryan had met their deaths from acute arsenic poisoning, and as a result of chemical analysis and other inquiries it had been established that arsenic was present in considerable quantity in their bodies and in the sausages which clearly were the cause of the poisoning.

"It is I think it is very clear that there must have been arsenic in Mr Martin's shop and that somehow or other it was introduced into the sausages in the process of their manufacture, but there is no evidence whatever as to how the arsenic got into the mixture nor how it came to be in the shop at all. I think the only verdict which I can return on the evidence is a formal verdict. I must confess I think the result is very unsatisfactory from the public point of view because not only have two valuable lives been lost but it appears that a great many other people in St Andrews were affected from the same source and it is perhaps fortunate that the death toll was limited to two people."

The poisoning affected over 150 people in St Andrews, killed two of its citizens and – I'm sorry to add – a dog that got fed three sausages.

Chapter 14

The Return of the 15th-Century Monks

In March 2012, sleepy St Andrews citizens living in the area of Greyfriars Garden were subject to the modern-day horror of being rudely awakened by the sound of pounding jackhammers on the road just outside their houses. The roadmen had a JCB standing by and trucks to remove the road waste as they continued a road resurfacing project that had worked its way down Market Street over the previous weeks. It was business as usual for the road crew, and they set themselves out for another busy day.

For the residents it was a ruined morning's sleep as the yellow-vested workmen laid into the road with machines and jackhammers with the unavoidable noise that unfortunately follows such a procedure. But after just an hour's work, there was a loud cry from the foreman to stop: "Stop the work immediately!"

Staring back at the workmen from the freshly excavated hole in the road was a human skull! After careful digging, an additional five full skeletons were revealed. It was time to down tools and bring in the archaeologists. This seemed a major find and Fife Council posted their top man, Douglas Speirs, to survey the dig and give it the care and attention it deserved. He stated, "I'm almost certain that these road workers have discovered part of a cemetery used by a small order of Franciscan friars around the 15th century. The exact setting of this place is not known but previous excavations in the area have failed to locate it. I strongly suspect that radiocarbon dating will fall into the period of 1458 to 1559, as we know from historical documentation that the friary was founded in 1458 and completed in 1478 under Archbishop Graham, and it was an early casualty of the Reformation, being ransacked in the year 1559."

A Franciscan friary was known to have existed somewhere in the near vicinity but exactly where had never been established. Members of the Franciscan order weren't buried in the nearby cemetery, but had their own little graveyard in the friary grounds.

In the area, recent installations of water, gas and electricity pipes and cables had produced nothing in the way of archaeology. This find here was being treated as unique, and careful analysis of the bones might reveal more about the lives of the Franciscan monks in St Andrews.

The Greyfriars area got its name from the monks, who traditionally wore the grey hooded costume of the order. The "grey friars" they were fondly regarded as collectively, and the name stuck.

The depth, or shallowness, of the skeletons came into question. This was answered by the archaeologists, who suggested that landscaping on the nearby houses had gone on before they were built and may have removed much of the top soil. Bodies were traditionally buried up to two metres deeper. Perhaps there was a mound that was removed, but my own observations in this area (me being a builder) make me think that very little landscaping would have been needed here: the surrounding area is flat.

My own suggestion is – going by the timescale given as 1458–1559 by the archaeologists – could these monks be some of the plague casualties that decimated the clergy in St Andrews? If we look back at my chapter on the plague in this book, one third of the ministry was wiped out in the year 1586 alone. That was a brutal lost year, but the plague had been active in Scotland for twenty years before that date. The archaeologists' end date is based on when the Catholic faith was driven out of St Andrews as a result of John Knox's fire and brimstone sermons.

The clergy died suddenly and fast with the plague. I feel that in the hurry to rid themselves of putrid corpses they buried them quickly and hastily. Further analysis showed the bodies had been partially burned, but of course this could have been done post burial before covering them over. The smell of a rotting corpse is bad enough, but a mass grave may require some burning – especially if the bodies are plague-ridden. I do feel these could be the remains of the clergy who took ill with the pestilence. Further excavation was concentrated on the area of the six skeletons, as it was deemed a burial ground, and evidence needed was adequate in the skeletons already disturbed.

When I spoke to Douglas Spiers recently, he gave his views of the dig and more information:

"The street the bodies were found on was built over in a construction of houses in the year 1840; what bodies we found consisted of four intact skeletons, a child's body aged between four or five, partial remains of a fifth, and over all 1,200 bones spread around the dig."

My previous books *Largo's Untold Stories* and *The Weem Witch* include some chapters on bones uncovered along the Fife coastline from Pictish burials to 16-century fishing folk. With the information I have gathered from these, I asked the archaeologist Douglas Spiers some questions:

Question 1 ... "Is there any way to determine how these individuals from the Greyfriars site died?"

Answer ... "No, not without further study. We had the timeline of the bodies from manuscripts written about the monastery, we for years just couldn't locate where the monastery was. With the finding of the skeletons it gave us the location we were looking for. A dig like this can be hugely expensive, and we just never had the funds to analyse the dig further, which was a shame."

Question 2 ... "What was the condition of the bones?"

Answer ... "Some were showing signs of wear and tear, the usual signs of a hard life, which was nothing new considering their age. The teeth were in a good condition. only showing the wear one would expect from a diet of mainly grains."

Question 3 ... "In my last book *Largo's Untold Stories* I cover two facial reconstructions, one from a Pictish burial ground, the other from an Arctic explorer from 1845. The Arctic explorer was identified as coming from Fife due to calcium tests that were done on his teeth. Was there thought to getting any such like tests on the Greyfriars monks?"

Answer ... "Again the expense on this is enormous, and we simply didn't have the funding to do this. You have to understand, we have found hundreds of skeletons around St Andrews and we simply can't afford such tests on all our sites. Although this site was important, we were holding up a building project and couldn't dwell on the time to do further testing."

Question 4 ... "Were there any metals found in the dig or evidence of coffins?"

Answer ... "No metals were ever recovered on the site or any evidence of coffins of any sort. What was found was evidence of a shroud being used to wrap the body up in it."

I was grateful for the interview but was saddened at the lack of resources and money that could have been spent here to make a facial reconstruction of one of the monks of old. Dundee University made a facial reconstruction of the Pictish woman described in my Largo book and it's now a tourist attraction in Dundee museum.

Chapter 15

Alphonse Capone "Scars" the Old Course

A few years back in London I was the acquaintance of a young girl who was deeply associated with the notorious Kray family in the East End of London. Her father had been a driver for the gangsters through their most famous period in the 60s and would be caught up as the police cracked down on the Krays' empire, arrested and jailed for a number of years, directly because of his involvement in the family's affairs.

That brings me to another famous gangster, this time with a connection to St Andrews ... would you believe Al Capone? There is indeed a St Andrews story about Capone, the 1920s Chicago hood who features in at least six major Hollywood films and is still as much a legend now as he was when he was alive!

Hit films featuring Al Capone and his violent lifestyle are as follows.

1959 ... *Some Like it Hot!*

1967 ... *The St Valentine's Day Massacre*

1983 ... *Scarface*

1991 ... *Oscar*

1975 ... *Capone*, and

1987 ... *The Untouchables*

(And I ought to add a record in my collection, a Motorhead EP with Girlschool called ... "The St Valentine's Day Massacre" ... which was brilliant!)

Capone was an enforcer, a gang boss, a vicious murderer who scaled the heights during the prohibition years in the United States, eventually amassing a personal fortune of 60 to 100 million dollars, which was an incredible sum in the 1920s, made from illegal alcohol smuggling, prostitution and racketeering. He used bribes and violence to impose forced sales on businesses, buying them at rock-bottom prices. If the buyer became difficult, Capone was known to blow up the shop or business. He killed over a hundred people with bombs placed in the businesses of those who refused to sell to him.

Although he was a ruthless gangster, those who knew him said he was also a kind and generous man, always helping the needy when he could. After his rise as a criminal boss he became famous as a Robin-Hood-like character, taking from the rich businesses in Chicago and opening soup kitchens free of charge to the needy and poor. He targeted police chiefs and politicians with heavy bribes to get them to turn a blind eye to his crime empire, and for a while everything he did was ignored.

But everything changed after a rival outfit – the North Side Gang – tried to muscle in on his empire. Al Capone carried out a calculated extermination of his enemies, taking out seven of the gang in the legendary "St Valentine's Day Massacre" at 2122 North Clark Street. They were lured to a garage used as a liquor distribution point, and all seven were machine-gunned down. This time the police had to act ... it was the beginning of the end for Capone's crime empire.

But let's start at the beginning, and tell the full story of this man and his connection to St Andrews ...

One of nine children, he was born Alphonse Gabriel Capone on 17 January 1899 in Brooklyn, New York City, to Italian parents.

His violent streak would surface at an early age – he was expelled from school for hitting a teacher full in the face. His early life saw him become active in joining urban gangs intent on violence and minor robberies. His first gang had the name of the Junior Forty Thieves; another was called the Bowery Boys. At 18 he was working as a bouncer at "Frankie Vale's Brooklyn Bar", a rather swanky, hot-spot nightclub, where a disagreement broke out between him and a client's girlfriend. The client, furious at an insult to his partner, pulled out a razor and sliced open the left side of Capone's face open. This was to give him a nickname that would make his legend in film and in life ... "Scarface".

To understand the background to his rise through the Brooklyn slums to enormous wealth, you need to look at America's political situation, with the austerity measures of its prohibition bill, which brought about a ban on sales of alcohol. The production and transportation of alcohol were made illegal after a campaign led by rural protestants in the Democratic and Republican political parties. It was made mandatory in the 18th amendment of the American Constitution, ratified in 1919.

The wartime Prohibition Act had banned the sale of alcohol to save grain for the war effort, but it was only passed in November 1918 – after the Armistice. With thousands of unemployed soldiers coming back from the war fields of France to mass unemployment it was decided to keep the prohibition law to keep violence off the streets.

Religious use of wines was allowed, but some states banned sales of alcohol outright.

With such strict measures imposed on the sale of alcohol, underground drinking and gambling dens rose, smuggled drink became big business with rampant demand, and Al Capone muscled himself in and took control.

Prohibition was designed to reduce crime but it had the reverse effect, establishing gangland criminal organizations at an alarming rate. Eventually politicians realised the helpless situation in policing such crime activities. They also saw the taxation that could be raised on alcohol, and it was decided to repeal prohibition, but it took till 1933 for the law to be changed by Franklin D Roosevelt's government, and by this time Al Capone had made his millions.

It wasn't the first time alcohol had been violently controversial in America. After the country gained independence the Whiskey Rebellion took place in Western Pennsylvania in 1791 in protest at the high taxes imposed on it ... the high tax was repealed after Thomas Jefferson became President in 1800.

Al Capone married in 1918 at the age of 19 to Mae Josephine Couchlin and the union produced a son, called Albert Frances (Sonny) Capone (1918–2004).

Capone worked as an enforcer for a Chicago brothel and found fame as a boxing promoter, but it would be the brothel that would be his eventual downfall ... infecting him with syphilis.

A bigtime gangster, "Big Jim Colosimo", was assassinated, and Al Capone was a chief suspect in the murder ... Capone and his friend Jonnie Torrio took over from the murdered Jim Colosimo and led the gang. It became a feared, Italian-based, terror gang. Other crime lords were either bought off or murdered, and Capone's group took the lion's share of alcohol bootlegging and prostitution in the city of Chicago, and big money started to roll in ... in no time Capone became a celebrity.

But now he was a crime boss, others wanted his title and business. In September 1926 he was ambushed in an assassination attempt. Several cars pulled up as he was sitting in a restaurant, the place was sprayed with machine-gun bullets, but they missed Capone. Twelve days later, his partner Jonnie Torrio was not so lucky. Shot several times by another assassin he pulled through surgery, but resigned his position as joint boss of the gang, leaving it all to Capone.

Al Capone immediately strengthened the group in an orgy of violence, attacking without mercy the rival gangsters he identified as the North Side Gang. Capone's personal driver had been taken off the street in broad daylight and tortured and murdered by his opponents, but a plan was in motion that would shatter the world of crime in its ruthlessness and ingenuity.

The St Valentine's Day Massacre, as it would come to be known, happened on 14 February 1929.

At 2122 North Clark Street in Chicago seven members of the North Side Gang arrived at a warehouse and garage at Dickens near Lincoln Park. Two policemen appeared and ushered the gang boys inside the warehouse. They were well-known hoods and leaders of the North Side Gang, accustomed to being harassed by police. They had no reason to suspect this was anything but a routine stop and search from the constables. But while they were lined up in the garage ready to be frisked by the policemen, two more men appeared, this time dressed in suits. Before any resistance could be offered, the policemen drew up submachine guns and along with the suited men sprayed the North Side boys with bullets.

Only one survived the shooting, Frank Gusenberg. He was shot with 14 bullets, but lived long enough to tell the police, "I'm not talking – nobody shot me!" A great defence from a man leaking from over a dozen bullet wounds. Gusenberg died in hospital.

Six more of the North Side Gang's main men had been assassinated ... Peter Gusenberg, Albert Weinshank, Adam Heyer, John May, Reinhardt Schwimmer and James Clark.

Two of the hit men would later fall foul of Capone. John Scalise and Albert Anselmi were later shot down. The word on the street was they were about to betray Capone, but his spies brought the news to him and he took immediate action to remedy the problem.

Al Capone's life would carry on till government officials caught him out in a tax scandal and managed to jail him at last. There is so much more to this man, but I hope you have the picture of a violent but clever man. His unlikely connection to this book about St Andrews is to do with his love of golf.

Capone was introduced to golf at the Burnham Woods golf course that lies eighteen miles from Chicago. He was instantly hooked on the sport.

His caddy reported he was absolutely useless at the sport, losing as many balls as the holes he played. He never once made par on any of the courses, but he was relaxed and jovial to all around him. Distanced from the weight of running his criminal empire, he could finally relax in the sport, though he still had a pack of armed men around him and a loaded gun in his golf bag! He was big on the betting of the game, with $500 being played on a hole. Sometimes he lost as much as $10,000 a game, which he was happy to pay out to the winners. He also paid his caddies extremely well: all of them thought he was a most generous man.

It is that reported the loaded gun in his golf bag went off one day, hitting his partner in the groin. Capone thought this hilarious, but there is no record of what Johnny Paton's thoughts were on his way to casualty!

Deirdre Marie Capone writes in her memoirs *Uncle Al Capone* that being Capone's grand-niece she remembers him travelling many times by ship to Scotland, with all his leading gang members, simply to play on the St Andrews Old Course. He would pay big money to professional golfers on the course to help his stroke. All were asked to keep their mouths shut as to the identity of their special guest. He had a St Andrews set of clubs specially made as he lorded it in St Andrews' best hotels, then had an engraver in the town put his initials on the handles of the set.

With a large bounty of $50,000 on his head from other Chicago crime lords, he talked to his grand-niece Deirdre about buying a house in St Andrews, with retirement and safety in mind. He was a huge lover of Scotch whisky, and Deirdre had no doubt that every time he stayed in St Andrews he was also making export deals with whisky bosses, for delivery to America.

But his plans for retirement in the home of golf were scuppered by the police and the Internal Revenue Service. In 1931 he was arrested – on charges of tax evasion. A lengthy trial found him guilty, and finally they jailed Capone for eleven years. He was released after eight years, but the syphilis he had contracted took a huge toll on his health, and he eventually died on 25 January 1947, to be buried in Mount Carmel Cemetery, Chicago.

It is fair to say that had the tax office not caught up with him he would very likely have made his home in St Andrews. The police and authorities had tried to nail him since the St Valentine's Day Massacre, but Capone was an expert in avoiding them and setting up alibis, always seen in public when his hoods were taking action on his behalf. They got him where he least expected it ... in unpaid taxes!

Chapter 16

The Return of St Andrew

On the restoration of the Catholic hierarchy in Scotland in 1878, Archbishop John Menzies Strain received from the Archbishop of Amalfi a large portion of the shoulder blade of the apostle St Andrew. It was taken from the tomb where all those years before a priest called Regulus had helped himself to the arm bones, kneecap and some fingers. It was placed in a glass and silver shrine and is held in high esteem in St Mary's Roman Catholic Cathedral in Edinburgh.

It was joined in 1982 by a further bone which had been given by Pope Paul VI to the newly created Cardinal Gordon Joseph Gray in 1969. Both relics can be seen in the Edinburgh cathedral today.

Of the whereabouts of the original St Andrew's bones brought by Regulus and his little party of monks and virgin nuns, nothing is known. But somewhere, some place, after John Knox's sermon in 1579, they were taken and hidden, maybe buried secretly, but whoever hid them took the secret to his deathbed ... they will probably remain hidden or lost for evermore.

Chapter 17

Today's St Andrews

Today St Andrews is still famed for its golf and university status. Dunino holds all its mystery of the druids' craft, and still is a haunting place to visit with its carvings on the cliff face, and sacrificial pool. The cathedral and castle are in a ruinous condition but it is great to visit and see the history that unfurled there, and in the graveyard can be found several graves here and there that show the occupant was drowned at sea and was another casualty from the fishing fleet. The bottle dungeon where many suffered can be seen at the castle, although it's caged off now and not accessible, which is a shame, but the mine and counter mine can be viewed and climbed in. You can also visualise from standing on the drawbridge and looking up to the window of the castle where David Beaton's body was once hung by his murderers.

The St Andrews Martyrs have a monument down from the castle but alas there's nothing to commemorate the many witches destroyed in St Andrews, which seems again to be forgotten about by most of the authorities in Scotland. It seems if you want to have a monument to commemorate the awful persecution these people went through you have to do it yourself, as I'm trying to do in Pittenweem for the accused witches in my first book *The*

Weem Witch. It's no surprise to note that it was lawyers who in 1736 brought about the end of the witch hunts, not ministers. Ministers voted against it! There were at least 1,400 witches destroyed in Scotland.

Robert Law in his *Memorials* writes that the repeal of the witchcraft laws offended the seceders from the Established Church of Scotland so much that their annual Confession of National and Personal Sins, printed in an Act of their Associate Presbytery at Edinburgh, 1743, lists among the "sins" the law tolerating Episcopalianism in Scotland, the law adjourning the Court of Session during Christmas holidays and "the Penal Statutes against Witches having been repealed by Parliament, contrary to the express law of God"!

Even today the church has a silent stance on any question of apologising towards the thousands upon thousands of witch hunts it pursued. Money can be found at the drop of a hat for protestant ministers' monuments, but the church finds it easy to forget the common men and women it accused as witches and destroyed. To me it reeks of double standards. I hope with awareness this can change. Any stone or monument today that has been built with the destroyed witches in mind has been done so with private money from relations of those who suffered.

My own relative Bessie Mason in 1644 was burnt as a witch in St Andrews.

St Andrews today is vibrant and full of tourists, and with its great pubs and restaurants, my favourite places to kill an afternoon are the antiquarian book shops where many of my library stock have come from to construct my previous works.

The harbour today is largely deserted, only a few lobster boats now, and several yachts – nothing like the trade it had in the 19th century, that cost so many wrecks and lost lives.

St Andrews is a wonderful place to visit today. I hope with this book I've answered some of your thoughts about this pretty city bathed in bloodshed and murders. Eighteenth-century writers felled forests producing book upon book of the hauntings and ghosts that had been seen in St Andrews, and with its gory history who can blame the place for having a ghost or five? But that's not for me to comment on.

All those years ago a very tall man with an iron handshake, called Uncle Fitz, took his niece's six-year-old boy round the castle and cathedral telling me their stories and secrets. Now with this book you can do the same!

Go on – keep this wonderful history alive!

Leonard Low ... 2015

Sources

A multitude of records has helped me to construct this book; my sources are as follows ...

The Gazetteer of Scotland, by Robert and William Chambers (1844)

The Kingdom: A Descriptive and Historical Handbook to Fife, edited by "Kilrounie" (1870)

The Register of the Kirk Session of St Andrews, part i, 1559–1582 (ed.) D.H. Fleming (1889)

The Register of the Kirk Session of St Andrews, part ii, 1583–1600 (ed.), D.H. Fleming (1890)

Wrecks and Reminiscences of St Andrews Bay, by George Bruce (1884)

Bygone Fife, from Culross to St. Andrews, by James Wilkie (1931)

Scottish Covenanter Stories: Tales from the Killing Time, by Dane Love (2005)

The Bass Rock, by W. Kennedy (1848)

Bygone Church Life in Scotland, by William Andrews (1899)

Anstruther, or Illustrations of Burgh Life, by George Gourlay (1888)

Fifiana or Memorials of the East of Fife, by M. F. Conolly (1869)

The Shores of Fife, by William Ballingall (1872)